Law of Attraction

Become A Wealth Magent And Manifest Future You Desire

(Harness Power Of Universe To Manifest Success, Money & Love)

Linda Penner

Published By **Elena Holly**

Linda Penner

All Rights Reserved

Law of Attraction: Become A Wealth Magent And Manifest Future You Desire (Harness Power Of Universe To Manifest Success, Money & Love)

ISBN 978-1-77485-584-3

No part of this guidebook shall be reproduced in any form without permission in writing from the publisher except in the case of brief quotations embodied in critical articles or reviews.

Legal & Disclaimer

The information contained in this ebook is not designed to replace or take the place of any form of medicine or professional medical advice. The information in this ebook has been provided for educational & entertainment purposes only.

The information contained in this book has been compiled from sources deemed reliable, and it is accurate to the best of the Author's knowledge; however, the Author cannot guarantee its accuracy and validity and cannot be held liable for any errors or omissions. Changes are periodically made to this book. You must consult your doctor or get professional medical advice before using any of the suggested remedies, techniques, or information in this book.

Upon using the information contained in this book, you agree to hold harmless the Author from and against any damages, costs, and expenses, including any legal fees potentially resulting from the application of any of the information provided by this guide. This disclaimer applies to any damages or injury caused by the use and application, whether directly or indirectly, of any advice or information presented, whether for breach of contract, tort, negligence, personal injury, criminal intent, or under any other cause of action.

You agree to accept all risks of using the information presented inside this book. You need to consult a professional medical practitioner in order to ensure you are both able and healthy enough to participate in this program.

Table of Contents

Chapter 1: What Is The Law Of Attraction? 1

Chapter 2: The Reasons So Many 9

Chapter 3: Loa And Relationships 12

Chapter 4: The Road That Leads To Possessions & Wealth 25

Chapter 5: Unlock The Power Of Intentionality 30

Chapter 6: Our Oyster Is The World 51

Chapter 7: Effective Techniques To Bring Success In Your Life 71

Chapter 8: The Birth Of The Law Of Attraction... 76

Chapter 9: Choice................................... 87

Chapter 10: What Are The Vibrations That May Be Holding You Back? 100

Chapter 11: Attracting And Fulfilling Your True Calling 115

Chapter 12: The Law Of Attraction....... 132

Chapter 13: What Is A Thought 147

Chapter 14: Harmony. Right Action. And Moving Your Body 158

Chapter 15: 'Force' The Universe To Give You What You Want 168

Chapter 16: Where Do I Start? 177

Chapter 17: Create The Love You Deserve 179

Conclusion 183

Chapter 1: What is the Law Of Attraction?

The law behind attraction is often misunderstood. Even though there is much false information about the law of attraction out there, the real power behind this phenomenon is often overlooked. It allows for you to manifest in your life what you are focusing upon.

The universal law known as the law of attraction is believed to be universal. It transcends religions and beliefs. It is active in all of our lives, regardless how much we understand it.

You can't just wish for everything. We would all be rich, famous, powerful and influential depending on what we choose. Although we would surely be surrounded with all that we want, this course will help you transform your life by teaching you how to use the law. It is, without doubt, life-changing when used correctly.

The universe, which is infinite and beautiful, is always changing. Everything around us is made of energy. Energy is constantly being transformed into new forms, and this is how we can best describe it. As other stars fade away, suns are emerging while others are becoming more prominent. Everything expands beyond a single point in time or space.

In the late 1960's, the hippy movement saw them write lyrics that claimed we were stardust. Every single element in life is a result of the stars. Even, inanimate objects.

We all ride the exact same waves of energies and they are flowing through each of us. It is incredible to realize how interconnected we are. Every event can influence every other but, unlike a ripple in a pond's water, we have the power and ability to shape our own futures.

A brief history about the law of attraction

If we accept that attraction is a universal law, it will have a long history. Both must have existed at once. Therefore, when we write history, it is common to mention when it was first recognised by mankind.

All we are is the outcome of what we have believed. The mind controls everything. We become what we think. - Buddha

One principle that runs through many religious beliefs is "What we think we're becoming". Hindus believe in Karma. This is the idea that what you do, or don't do, will eventually result in your own good. This idea is also implied in passages from the Christian Bible.

He shall reap what he sows.

Karma is used in every day conversation in Western societies. However, we don't usually think too much about the philosophy or the history. Yet, many believe it has some power.

These words were written 19th century by Thomas Troward.

Thought precedes tangible form. If left alone, the nucleus will attract all the conditions necessary to become visible in the outside world.

Here, we see that he clearly understands and depicts elements of the law-of-attraction and how manifestation can become a creative component. James Allen and Lilly followed his lead, writing a series of books, articles and books between 1901-1912. The most renowned is "As an Man Thinketh."

William Walker Atkinson published a book entitled "Thought Vibration/The law of Attraction: In the Thought World". This was the first mention of the terms law of attraction.

This method of thinking was seen as a new wave. Wallace Wattles was another person who thought in this way. He published the book "The Science of Getting Rich." Wallace incorporated these principles into his own lives by creating imaginative visualizations. He would visualize the vision in his mind and then move towards it.

Napoleon Hill's 1937 bestseller "Think and Grow Rich", which sold a million copies, was the moment when the law of attraction gained popularity. This book is considered a classic today, in the selfdevelopment niche. Hill was particularly interested in how to control your thoughts and achieve success. He was also a key influence on "The Secret", the popular movie.

Uell S. Anderson, a self help author, wrote a book titled "Three Magic Words", later renamed to "The Key to Power to Personal Peace." This meant that each outcome can be created by you and you are the creator of your world. This way was becoming increasingly popular, but many people have never understood the core roots that hold it all together.

If we look back at this short history, we can see that the main principles have always been running through many great thinkers minds. The fact that many other areas, including religion and free spirit thinking, have linked into the law o attraction shows that there is something truly powerful at the core.

Can we apply the law to our everyday lives?

In all walks of our lives, the principle of "like attracts kind" is evident. While you might hear the term "opposites attract" when talking about relationships, it is actually true that we tend be attracted if we are very similar. But, it is not uncommon to see abusive relationships attract more people. If the victim believes that they have everything, then they may be giving off signals that invite more of the same. Although this is not their fault they can make changes.

When we use the expression "Money comes to money," it is often used to refer to someone who has already been rich but appears to have just received another financial windfall. This is often done in an envy-driven way that can later be seen to be working against the speaker as it relates to what he/she would like. Money does not always go to money, but it is true according to the basic law that attracts.

Someone who is used and comfortable with having money will have a tendency to think like someone who sees only wealth. This makes it more likely that they will manifest more of what their already have. This happens naturally and doesn't require any additional learning.

An individual who is unkind to others by being rude, obnoxious or anti-social can often be a person living in envy. This is a rare way to be happy. Although they may still experience some good fortune, they tend to concentrate on the negative aspects of their lives. You may have heard the expression, "Oh, he is only happy if he feels miserable". This indicates a person who has a tendency to think negatively and is stuck in an unsustainable routine. This leads to a self-destructive cycle and attracts more.

Someone who smiles and sees the good in everyone is the opposite. This way of thinking does not guarantee happiness. However, it increases the likelihood that happiness will manifest in the individual's life. A good example of this is how others might come to the person's rescue or invite them into the social circle. This person is likely be more connected to their friends and have more interests. All the above are examples that the law of attraction works, even though we don't know the real power behind them. So the natural laws that govern attraction do not need to be manipulated.

Chapter 2: The Reasons So Many

Many successful people have mastered the art of manifesting the ideal reality. It took those who were priviledged to learn the true secrets of manifesting to take the time necessary to understand their nature and the natures reality.

Although the law is well-known, few people fully understand why it works and why it fails. This is similar to praying, where some people get instant miracles while others struggle to pay the bills. If you want to manifest what you want, it is important to understand how you can align yourself with power. Only then can you attract what you have in your mind and repeat with affirmations.

There are many Laws of Attraction courses that will teach you the best affirmations to use and help you change things about yourself. You've been told that changing one quality in yourself is enough to make things work. But, even after working for months to improve one particular quality about yourself, you discover that it is still very difficult.

Attunement is all about aligning with your inner source. There is no way around it. You can think of your computer now as an appliance. This computer can have all the software and languages that it needs, but it cannot function if the circuits are not turned on. You are no more than a human being.

Even though affirmations may have helped many people over the years, just imagine what would happen if the source could be connected to you like a computer. That source of power can be called God, Universe, or anything else we like. But what really matters is that we have all that is needed.

Connecting to that source changes your biology and opens up the doors to achieving your goals. What happens to your life after you have stopped trying to be or do the things you want will be miracles.

To calm your mind and body, first, lie down and relax. Next breathe in through the nose. Now focus on the breath.

Once you have experienced the desire you feel, you can visualize that feeling in your mind.

The feeling you desire is what you can capture. What would you feel if you had achieved your dream? The visualization helps you to visualize your desired outcome.

These techniques are easy to use and will make miracles come true in your life.

The law of attraction, along with many other spiritual laws, was something that ancients understood. How can you connect to your source of power so that you get the results you desire? True manifestation is the way you live your lives.

Chapter 3: Loa and Relationships

LoA, love and affection

Most likely, the law is not yours on your first date.

It's easy to see how it applies for love and relationships. You might instead view it as a tool for extracting material wealth from the universe.

LoA can have a lot of things to do with relationships. The LoA offers guidance about how to approach potential partner outside of relationships and also suggests ways to interact with them inside relationships. We'll be discussing how LoA can work in your romantic relationship.

Finding the right individual

When you look at the LoA for more then a few minutes it will become obvious how it is recommended that you find "the right" person. Instead of obsessing on someone you don't like or jumping into a romantic relationship with the first person you meet, think about who you are.

It is worth taking the time to reflect on this. Think about this person. If this is you,

Have you ever had very similar interests as yours? Oder if they have very similar interests?

Are you interested in sharing your interests with someone else?

These questions are important to answer and you can incorporate them in your visualization. Then, imagine how you will meet this person. You will meet them at work. Do you want to meet at a religious service? Is it possible to meet at the conference which relates to your passions? Then, fix your ideas and focus on making plans.

Even though you may not feel an immediate connection, something may begin to happen. Your appearance will become less important when you are interacting with potential partners. Instead, your focus should be on your vision. You will quickly be able recall what you desired and identify whether the person is a good match.

Furthermore, once you find the right person to fulfill your vision, it will be obvious to you that this is who you really want to be with. Instead of being nervous at the thought of asking him or her out on date, you will feel confident that your decision was correct and will not have any trouble making it happen.

How to improve romance relationships

The LoA also makes suggestions regarding romantic relationships. We say that negotiation is an essential part any relationship. We assume that if we fail to find ways to make our partner a debtor to us, they will never do anything for me.

Unfortunately, it can lead to unhappy relationships. Today we may be able do something to benefit our partner. Tomorrow we may have to do something else.

Instead, we can follow LoA's advice to break free of this cycle. It is important to do good things for your partner, without asking for or expecting any reciprocity.

At first, it may be difficult to do these things. You might find yourself washing dishes and cleaning the house more than you wanted. You'll eventually feel proud of your selfless act and want to repeat it.

Importantly, when your partner notices you doing this, he/she will want to reciprocate and do something for you. This positive circle can dramatically improve the quality and happiness of your relationship. It will also help you stop making the same mistakes that so many people make in relationships.

How to deal if relationships do not work

At times in our lives we may find ourselves in relationships which are not meant to. The beliefs of your future spouse could be diametrically opposite. You may even want to pursue completely incompatible goals.

As time goes by, relationships can turn into a sham. You might end up fighting over trivialities with someone you once considered a potential friend. We choose to stay together and move on with our lives. Instead, we are bitter and leave the relationship in a poor state.

The LoA allows us to see that there is a way out of a bitter breakup. Instead of dwelling on the possibility that things will get worse or that the breakup is inevitable, we can choose to focus on something other than that.

We can put our efforts into the relationship ending. It is possible to imagine how we can end the relationship, without becoming bitter or hurting other people's feelings. While it might sound different, it's possible to end your relationship without resentment. It can be done in cordial, friendly ways.

How to move past a failed relationship

We've all had to share in the disappointment of a relationship ending. The other person may not be the right person for us, but we are truly in love with them.

This can be very distressing and some people may not fully recover for years. If this is you, it is important that you remember the LoA. Positive thoughts attract positive effects and negative ones attract negative outcomes.

If you are only focusing on the loss of the loved one you once loved, you will only be attracting more negativity. You will become more negative and more focused upon the person who is no part of you.

Instead, you should focus on the recovery, stabilization, and finding ways to fill in the void left after a person leaves. You can take a break from your relationship and set goals that relate to work. Another option is to focus on finding a replacement partner.

No matter what you do or how you approach it, you must remember the lessons of LoA. Instead of worrying about the future and dwelling on how you might never get it back, think positive thoughts.

Friendships

LoA has more to share about friendships. It provides advice on how you should behave in romantic relationships and also offers suggestions on what you might be doing wrong when it comes to friendships.

While your instinctive reaction may be to think you are doing nothing wrong with your friends, it might not be the best idea. If you take the time to really consider this, you might discover a completely different conclusion. Take a look at all the friendships you have lost over the years that were supportive, kind, caring. What if you lost those friends? Then again, your life is not going to be the same if these friends have never left you. The LoA gives us some guidelines for making and keeping friends.

a. Making friends

The LoA is extremely specific in how it suggests that you make friends. Instead of suggesting you should simply fall into friendships without planning, the LoA encourages you to focus and visualize your goals.

Instead of waiting for friends to appear, set goals. First, decide you want to make friends. Second, consider who they might be. Will they share similar jobs? Will they have the same education and training? Will they be able and willing to help in any way? Will they be able respond in kind to your request?

Focusing on the goal and answering the questions will help you focus and visualize. Imagine these friends entering your life, meeting you and engaging in daily activities with them.

Consider including people you meet in your visualizations. Imagine what role they play in your life. What do they do to make your life better? Do they make me a better person? Do they help you do things you couldn't do otherwise?

However, this information may not be available in advance. Learning more about someone can help you understand their contribution to your life. You might have to think about what you want and then make decisions.

Be aware that the LoA would also suggest that you go through this process for any existing friends. You may not have known this person for a long while but that does not make them a positive influence in their lives.

If you see yourself improving with the negativity in a friend's life, then you can either encourage them to become more positive yourself or try to distance yourself so that you do not become more negative.

b. How to connect with friends

Not only should you be looking for friends, but you also need to use LoA to strengthen and evaluate existing relationships. As you probably know, if friendship is not nurtured and maintained, you can drift apart.

To visualize the results of your friends, you'll need to use LoA. Focusing on some friends can help to build lasting friendships. Don't forget to consider who doesn't have an important role or who plays an excessively negative role in your daily life.

Decide who you want and what you are not comfortable with. Also, consider who you should avoid. To visualize the changes in your relationships, you can use the power and flexibility of visualization.

Consider how much you might be able to avoid negative friends. Or think about how you can interact constructively with them.

Positive roles in your life are only. But, no matter what decision you make, don't imagine yourself in this situation.

If you're looking for friends to get in touch with, consider ways you can work together.

Instead of seeing them as a small part of your daily life, focus on what you can do to make your relationship more positive.

c. Rebuilding broken relationships

Finally, the LoA offers a lot of advice for broken relationships. LoA is a good tool to use in situations where you have had a disagreement or want to make amends.

You should always start with the end in mind, which is to restore your broken relationship. Then think about how you will achieve it. You will call your friend and apologize for anything you have done. Will you apologize for something you did?

Imagine the entire process. Imagine what the process will look like, how you might respond to it and how you will get there.

Bring your abundance mindset with you to any meeting with an old friend. Do not expect to win a battle over words. Do not assume victory in the previous position or belief.

Instead, think about your goal: To get your friend's back. So it goes.

Visualization, focus and tracking can help you achieve it.

Remember the last stage in the LoA: You must be open and prepared to accept the results. If you ever doubt that you want your friend back, then you can destroy the goal before you have the chance to reach it.

Summary

We've provided a thorough overview of the Law of Attraction as it relates to relationships in this chapter. LoA contains very detailed instructions about what to do, regardless of whether you are dealing with a strained romantic relationship or a broken friendship.

I have already mentioned two things in this chapter: The first, and most common of all LoA applications, is the three-step procedure.

Step # 1. Think about what it is that you really want. Step # 1: Think about what you really want. In this instance, it could be to repair a broken friendship or ending a relationship.

Step #2: Visualize what you will see each day. This could involve imagining your spouse: who will he/she be? Where will he/she work? What kind of background will they have?

Step #3: Let the result come to you - that's step

Your spouse to make new friends or fix a damaged friendship. We are often our worst enemies when it comes to receiving the things that we believe we need.

We unconsciously push them aside when they are finally in reach. This is against the LoA's advice.

Along with the three-step process, it's important to have a mentality based on abundance wherever you do LoA. Instead of worrying about whether you will "lose" a friendship or romantic partner, consider what you can win by creating a mutually beneficial environment.

Chapter 4: The Road that Leads to Possessions & Wealth

The path you choose to take to the future might seem unknowable. It's just uncertain because it hasn't happened yet. The life you have lived so far is a testament to your ability to handle the many years of success. You can see the success of others around you and wonder why your life isn't as full and rewarding. Some people seem to be able to do everything while you struggle. You may blame your situation. You may see your situation as one of the most difficult in your life. However, the Law of Attraction can be applied to anyone. They just need the ability to use it.

Knowing your goals will help you be more successful in your endeavors. While there are many people who have vague goals, they rarely come to pass. It's not like you want something badly enough to feel that you can have it. To attract good things, you must have a detailed plan.

A 52 inch TV screen is what you want, but you aren't sure your resources will allow it. It is putting obstacles in your path. While this doesn't mean you should ignore your commitments and buy one, it does mean you have to follow the steps in this chapter. It works for everyone. It's possible to achieve what you want if your imagination can see it.

How thinking works

Because they know where and what they want. Some may choose a new vehicle. Some may own a whole CD collection, while others may simply want to be rich. But if the picture isn't clear, then other things will take priority. Look closely at the object that you are pursuing. Focus on the details and stay firm in your resolve to acquire whatever it is you want.

The price. Knowing what you must do to get it is key. If you are determined to own the thing you desire, obstacles will be put in your path and you will find a way.

It's not like you know what you want, but you are unable to get it. While you might not be able to identify what those things are, it's clear that others are getting more than yours. If you truly see and know what you want, then you have a goal. When you think positively about that goal, you'll find that your priorities change so you can get the thing that is important to you.

How does it work to get rich?

Rich is possible for everyone. All people have the same opportunity. The problem is that everyone doesn't have a clear picture about what makes them rich. If you don't know the destination of your car, it is very unlikely you will make it there. The same holds true for wealth. It only works if you know how wealthy you want to become. Once you have established your goals, you will find you know where you are heading and can alter your life to meet those goals. This is where people who achieve are different from those who fail.

Here are some examples from people who have succeeded

Richard Branson was a multimillionaire entrepreneur and wrote a book called, "Screw It. Let's do It." This book explained the Law of Attraction. They didn't always have plenty of money. He set himself clear goals, and he did what he wanted to do. His most important questions were:

What do YOU want?

Who am i?

How will I do it?

This was because he answered these questions definitively and was able to make a lot of money. Everyone has the opportunity to do the same. He didn't start rich. He didn't start from nothing but an idea. Microsoft's entrepreneur had a similar attitude. Bill Gates knew who and what was possible. He also knew exactly what he wanted and how to get there. This will allow you to conquer the world. This doesn't mean that you are going to be happy. You won't be happy, but happiness and good relationships with others do come into play. This is covered in a chapter.

Chapter 5: Unlock the Power of Intentionality

As I stated in the previous chapter you can see the results of taking action on your goals, no matter what they are. You will see that your actions can have a profound impact on your reality.

This gives you confidence, so you can take more actions. Not all of them are going to succeed, but enough will give you confidence. This creates a downward spiral. By taking more actions, you can become more confident. This, in turn, will allow you to take even greater action.

You'll soon notice that your reality changes. This is how your path changes. Simply draw a map of your journey and start walking.

So far so good, right?

Many people end up tripping when they try to walk the path that will lead to the life they desire. Some get lost. Others get distracted and disoriented by the potholes.

This is a shame because everyone has hopes and dreams, but few of them are actually able to come true.

As I have said, the Law of Attraction can already work in your favor. Whatever you are focusing on grows.

Intentionality is the key to unlocking this reality.

The solution is right in front of you

As I said in the chapter, desire is external. It cannot be triggered by things they don't control.

These are external triggers. This puts you in a bizarre position where you believe that things will work out for your desires.

The trigger isn't located outside of your body. Instead, you are the one who triggers your desire.

In this chapter I will guide you through a simple exercise which would allow you to harness the power to desire whenever you wish, wherever you wish.

But I need to make it clear that you cannot rely solely on external triggers.

First, the right thing doesn't always come at the right timing. Sometimes, inspiration comes in unexpected forms when you need it.

Maybe it's not enough. It could be too late. It doesn't always happen as quickly as you would hope.

These are just some of the reasons it's not worth waiting to see if external triggers will help you unleash the power and desire in your life. It's going to take more initiative

The Solution: Be INTENTIONAL

Certain energies and realities attract you. You may not like the results you have attracted. You are unhappy at one level or another with your current life.

You're right. Here's how I can help you change that. It's possible to attract the reality you desire simply by being more intentional.

Visualization's Power

All that is required to achieve intentionality is clarity about what you are really looking for. Although it may sound straightforward, most people aren't clear on what they desire.

They desire to have the best life they can. They wish to have a wonderful relationship. They wish to have a rewarding career. That's exactly what they claim.

When you really pay attention to what their emotions are and what they do, it's easy to see how they can be quite inconsistent. Many times they contradict their own statements. They seem lost, confused, and just wander around in circles. They live in a confused fog.

Intentionality, in which you visualize what you want, is the opposite. As I said before, visualizing your dream must be broken down into specific goals.

This is essential because you can make things happen if you choose to live your life in a way that is consistent with your ideal reality. You are not dependent on other people changing. You aren't waiting for the rest of the world to take a break. It's not your job to do this.

Instead, concentrate on the intense desires you feel. Allow this to flow through you. You can then do what you need to make your dreams come true for you and your loved ones.

This is where visualization comes in. You can't claim you are looking for something based upon a guess, a theory, and/or some type of fuzzy mental image.

Instead, visualize your dream reality down to its smallest details.

As I've said before, when discussing goals, you need to recall and repeatedly recite the "who, who, what, where and when" acronym.

Intentionally Make Your Visualized Reality Yours

A lot people see their big dreams and goals as episodic goals. I mean that they will only contemplate their grand vision for life when they feel they have the time or space. Sometimes they wait for people to ask what their big ambitions might be.

You lose track of key details when you wait to see those special moments. The more time you put off telling people or reminding yourself about your big dreams, the less powerful they become. It is no longer something you would be willing to sacrifice everything for.

I promise you, most people have a to-do list.

I should lose some weight.

I should quit smoking.

I should exercise.

I need to increase my skills.

I should. The list could go on.

You can't forget your grand vision and it becomes another task on your to-do lists.

Intentional Living: A Repeated Choice

An ancient Greek philosopher once said "We are all what we do repeatedly." While he was talking specifically about excellence and other virtues but the same concept still applies to how we choose and live our lives. His point about choosing an action to do and then repeating until it becomes habitual is his point.

You will not be able choose to spend your time pursuing the life you dream of. You are focusing your attention on something else, which is reflected in every aspect of your day.

Instead of focusing on what you don't want, turn it around and focus on what is important to you. Detail it. Allow yourself emotional transport to the alternate reality.

How would you feel?

What would it be like to see?

What would you do to fulfill your desires?

Would you consider thinking differently?

What would your current train of thought look like?

How would the world view you?

How will you define yourself in such a world?

Where is it?

How would the world look at you in such a setting?

Ask yourself these questions, and other related ones. Be in this place, both mentally and emotionally.

Visualize Your Results

Imagine your dreams coming true. And now you live your dream.

What does that reality look like? It should be described in concrete terms.

Which address are you at?

Which kind of house do your family live in?

What does it look, you ask?

What are its unique features?

Who do you hang with?

What do people think of you?

You can accept this as your reality. Let yourself feel like you are taking it for granted. This is your everyday, daily reality.

Do not Forget to Take The Next Step

You now have the strong visualization of an alternate reality in your mind. This is what you can smell, feel, touch, hear, see and do. The next step is to return to the life stage that you were before reaching your ideal reality.

I'm referring here to the long period of time between now and where we want to be.

Make a mental picture of all the sacrifices necessary. Imagine the work you had to do.

Is it possible to live your dreams?

Were you patient?

Did your gaze stay on the prize, or were you distracted?

Did you give up your time and enjoyment in order to reach your goals? What kinds of setbacks were you able to overcome?

How did these difficulties overcome?

This step is often overlooked by people who want to tap the power of Law of Attraction. This is why many people fail.

They cannot see what happens in between. This is essential because it prepares them for the ups-and-downs, twists/turns, and detours of their path to success.

If you focus only on the end stage, you won't be prepared for what lies ahead. For you to have the life you desire, you must also think about the things you need to do and the people you need.

Visualize the Worst-Case Scenario. And your Victory over It

What's the worst that can happen when you try to put your best foot forward in reaching your ultimate goal. Imagine it happening.

Now, imagine yourself trying your best to overcome this obstacle.

At first it may feel difficult. But you will eventually get the hang of it as you keep doing this mental exercise. It is important to notice that your attitude begins to shift.

It's a common occurrence that if you don't get the front door, the backdoor, the sidedoor, or the basement working, you have the option of trying the next day. If all fails, you can always try the next day.

You are building strength. You are also tapping into intuition.

Finally, emotional perseverance is developed by continually repeating scenarios in your mind and visualizing the end goal.

These setbacks won't be a problem if and when they do occur. You don't get into an emotional tailspin that makes you feel like everything you've done for your personal life has been a huge waste.

Instead, things are going according to plan. You don't feel any emotional reaction.

Instead, the hit happens suddenly and you bounce up as if it never happened. You learn from what you have done and you continue trying.

It happens again.

Affirmations: Increase your Intelligence and Power Through Affirmations

Based on what your imagination tells you, you will get an idea about who you really are. Ask yourself this question: "Whom am I?" Where am I going to go? What am I capable to do? What kind are you?

This is not the place to stop your visualization. This is where your vision becomes a reality and the world's success becomes a reality.

I also want to mention the middle of your journey between where are you now and where do you need to be.

Ask yourself the following question: "Whom am I?" What's my goal? What am I capable to do? What kind of person is I?

Once you have visualised the worst-case scenario and how you overcome them you should ask yourself these question: "Who am I?" Is this really where I am going? What am i really capable of doing? What kind are you?

It is important to note that I didn't invite you to ask me questions about the opinions of others. It doesn't make any difference. I did not ask anything about your past. They don't define what you are.

Instead, I urge you to visualize all of the frustrations, setbacks or challenges you faced while you were moving from where your are to where you want to be.

While you are doing visualization exercises, repeatedly ask these questions. It is possible to observe that your answers change. Expect it.

Once you have nailed down the adversity for the future, the most important thing is to reach a place of clarity. This will make you mentally prepared for any adversity that may come your way.

Do your best to be the best version you can be

Based on where your goal is and what challenges you face along the way, make an affirmation that really cements who and what you are. Recite these daily.

Different people will come up with different affirmations. Everyone comes from different backgrounds. We phrase things differently.

It is crucial that you create affirmations that make sense to your heart. These are statements of fact.

One example is:

I am strong.

I am available for whatever life throws at us.

I'm never surprised because my mind is always ready.

My past does not define me.

I am always learning.

I know that I will conquer any challenge.

Because I have learned from the mistakes of the past, I am victorious.

You can create your own variations. What's most important is the emotional content of such statements. They must be able to reach your heart and bring out the desire and intention. These statements reflect your reality.

It's not the same thing that your parents said. You aren't repeating things that your relatives, friends or others in your social network usually say. You are the only one who can say these things, and you must have them come from your heart.

This may sound difficult at first. The statements are so out of step with your reality. There seems to have been a disconnect.

However, the more that you believe, feel and repeat them, the stronger the results.

Slow down and practice pairing visualizations with each of your affirmation statements

It's easy to say, "I am strong," when you think of yourself. Think of a time when you are forced to be stronger. It's not enough to say that as a mantra.

This should be tied to an image that shows you overcoming something. Recall a time when you faced problems in the past.

In fact, before you can imagine the future, it is a good idea to first reflect on your past. The wonderful thing about your history is that it has already taken place. You already have the ability to do it because you have done it before.

No matter how strong your affirmation sentences may sound, take a moment to slow down and link them with a visualisation or a memory from the past.

Dig Deep

Whatever you do when visualizing a past, future, or other event, keep your eyes on the sights, sounds, and smells. You can do this while you focus on the inner voice and recite your affirmations.

Believe and Assume.

If you're using affirmations to affirm your beliefs, you should believe that your affirmation is true. "I am strong" should be your affirmation. You must own it. That strength is not something that's going to happen in future.

It is who you really are, right where you are. You can confidently assume you are strong enough by believing it.

This time, connect it to visualizing your past or future. Whatever the case, it is important to feel its reality.

This should be done every day. This is not something you should save for the future. This exercise should not be repeated more than once in a lifetime.

Instead, you should incorporate intentional visualization and desire awakening using affirmations into your daily routine. You can take it as little as 10 minutes, fifteen minutes, or even more. It's completely up to the individual.

Make it part of every day.

Meditation and Mindfulness can help you to boost your visualization skills.

There are many books and articles on medication and mindfulness that you can find on the Internet. I won't waste time listing what they are.

For maximum mental focus, it is important to practice mindfulness and meditation. Both can be used to help you feel present and in control.

Meditating or practicing mindfulness can help you forget the past. It will not cause you to feel sad or anxious. You learn to focus and not be emotionally activated when you do this.

Because these are powerful skills mindfulness or meditation can help to increase the power and effectiveness of your visualization. Without getting emotional or distracted, you can acknowledge your thoughts. You can visualize the future you want more clearly and brighter.

If mindfulness and meditation are a regular part in your daily life, you can achieve your desired reality.

It is instead a reality that can be seen, heard, touched, tasted, and smelled with your mind. Also, it is not a long shot. Your target is right in front of you. It doesn't take much effort for you to see and feel it.

Be conscious of the road you're taking

The road ahead of you must lead you to the destination you desire. This means that your goal should be possible to deconstruct. This point should help you to be able accomplish that.

Next, separate the goals into subgoals. This will allow you to set deadlines for your subgoals.

You can then break these goals down into smaller tasks you can complete on a daily basis. These are your daily tasks.

Now, look at what you have already written.

Is it possible to draw a straight line between what you do daily and where you want to go? If not, continue to work on your list. It has to be simple.

This must be the roadmap of your life, which you should start right away.

Similarly, your thoughts need to be mapped towards your ultimate goal.

Ask yourself: "Is it clear that there is a relationship between what I think about each day and how I view them. What about the kind of work I should be doing to achieve the goals I have set for myself?

Changes can be made if necessary.

You need to have a clear connection between your thoughts and your ability, right here and now, to do deep work. All of these goals add up to your ultimate objective.

Chapter 6: Our Oyster is the World

There is no such thing, "Perfect" in this World.

It is hard to stress enough the lessons we've learned over the years.

The Story of the Comb

A young man of wealth was once asked which was his most valuable possession.

He took out an antique comb with some missing teeth from his pocket.

Everyone who had ever met the wealthy young man were puzzled, but he explained.

"This comb reminds of me that nothing is perfect in this world. I prefer to find meaning and gratitude for what is here and not there than to grieve about it.

There is no substitute in knowing yourself, and knowing what will make our lives happy.

Also, one can have what he or she wants, but what one needs and wants are the same as those of others.

The exercises of the previous morning taught us that our 21-day journey toward a better life and happier lives is based on knowing ourselves and others.

Do Something New, Something Good For Others

Days One through Ten have been fun and you are on a roll.

Do not be afraid to go a step further.

Your journey has shown you there are many options for how you can grow into a stronger, happier, and more successful version of yourself.

You can learn something new. It's never too late, after all, to learn a new skill.

You will be halfway through your 21 day journey to a better you.

You might plant a seedling or grow an herb farm to get your constant supply of fresh ingredients.

You could also begin a vegetable or fruit garden, which would help to start a semivegetarian lifestyle.

If you live near a forest, you have the option of planting a new tree there.

Depending on your personal needs and interests, you can have a plant garden or a healing garden.

Tiling the soil can bring us many benefits such as more food security when our produce is grown. The additional benefit of cultivating a garden is the ability to communicate with nature.

Also, Mother Earth benefits from your own gardening. Your carbon footprint is reduced when you eat less meat and this reduces the damage to the ozone layers.

Doing good for others is possible by volunteering at your local orphanage, senior home or pet shelter.

Do-gooding will bring you a lot of good Karma.

But it's not like that.

Do good without waiting to be rewarded.

Good deeds that help others are already the reward.

We are too short to dwell on the things we wish we could have done.

Do it!

Bring your bags and see the World

Day Twelve has you packing all the necessary travel gear and getting your bags packed.

Even after all of our life lessons over the last 11 days we may be stumped when the question is asked, "Why do people travel?"

Even when the obvious answers seem obvious.

To start, we need to ask the more fundamental question: "What is your motivation for traveling?"

Travel can be defined in the dictionary as a variety of things.

Travel means to travel. For some, travel seems to be more of a necessity than an option or luxury.

Let us forget the notion of travelling being a vacation or tour we are going to do each year, or our lifelong dream to travel the world.

Many people make their living traveling.

This type is also known as "just moving or going to one place from another" and it can be interpreted as such:

There are salespeople who need to hop on a plane or bus to get to their destination.

They see travelling as a necessity, or part of their job.

These people are unable to make a living from their travels.

The same holds true for all people in the travel and commercial industries.

The many people who make up the air, sea, or maritime, metro railroads and any vessel that transports people over short distances or long distances.

There are those who travel not for the money, but because they must.

These include students who have the need to travel from their school to their school, daily, monthly, or for an entire academic year.

Not only are those who need travel to meet their needs, but so do those who are forced to.

This is the best reason not to travel.

To take home the remains or say goodbye to a family member is the most terrible reason to travel long distances.

Let's now get to the fun reasons people travel.

Many people travel to enjoy their leisure time.

When you mention the word "travel", first thoughts are of sunbathing on a sandy beach, gazing up at Eiffel Tower, or skipping down the Himalayan snowy slopes.

However, there are many options for leisure and recreational travel.

It is not difficult to find literature or information on this type of travel.

There has been so much written, that one wonders "Why?"

This humble piece is about why we travel. It's my humble opinion on why humanity seems to want to travel from one place, when it's possible to stay at home, and avoid any danger or inconvenience that might occur.

Many people pack their suitcases, passports, and visas just to escape on a short or long vacation.

They desire a fun time that is easygoing, free from all the hustle and bustle of their daily lives.

They just want to get out of it all, regardless of whether they plan to explore the entire globe or only for a few days.

Some people travel simply to escape.

There are people who seek relief from the many hardships of life.

It is possible to say that this type if traveler travels to escape reality, or just to live.

Then, there is the group of people who are starting to explore. Wanderers, if your heart desires. They are easily bitten and can't seem shake the wanderlust bug.

Lucky people have the opportunity to make a career and vocation from it.

Sometimes luck smiles on those who get paid for their travels around the globe.

For these types of travellers, there is still an occupational danger. That is the danger presented each time you board a plane, boat, or any other type of transport.

However, it is a chance that anyone can take when they fly or travel by bus or plane anywhere in the world.

This increases the risk exponentially if it is done on a regular or daily basis.

Even more so if you are part of a crew of journalists covering war-torn areas or places at risk of terrorist attacks.

The risk of leaving the safety and comforts at home for any reason is one that you take.

Many adventurers enjoy endless adventures in unknown territory and the thrill of going on safari in Africa's wild deserts.

Some might argue that these experienced adventurers are able to take leisure travel up a notch.

Those who prefer to be safe in their own homes can still get the best of what the rest of the world has to give.

These are those we may refer to as armchair travellers.

They can also surf in the wild or go on a hunting expedition with the help internet cable TV.

It does not require that you leave your comfort zone or pay a lot of money in order to enjoy sight-seeing and learn about another culture.

So, despite all the writings that have been made about why people travel it all comes down to the human nature of each person. The need to escape from reality at any given moment and to be somewhere else is what drives us.

To travel is to leave one's current world in search of a better, more permanent one.

Now you have the opportunity to explore the rest of the world, including Paris, Paris or other destinations, and the whole world.

After all, it's a way to live.

Nurturing Your Child in Every Single One of Us

Every parent wants their children to be successful.

We do our best every day to offer our children the same opportunities as we have.

We work card to offer them education, and we pray that their futures will be better than ours.

We all know that we are a product of all the experiences in our lives since birth.

From the moment that we gain consciousness, and even earlier according to scientific studies to this effect, our minds have been shaped and shaped by the experiences and knowledge we have gained up to now.

These experiences, good and bad, are a sum total of who we have become and how our reactions to each day's events.

How do we ensure that our dreams are realized for our children?

Our role as parents and educators to our children is crucial.

Each of us have different ways of disciplining and training our children. But we need to find ways to give our children and all children around the world the opportunity to learn and grow in a safe environment that encourages them to be kind and helpful to others.

As parents and potential parents, it should be our deepest wish that we are able to raise a new generation which will not only make us proud but also reflect our dreams.

Thus comes to mind the poem we likely all learned in preschool.

CHILDREN LEARN ABOUT THE WAYS IN CHILDREN LIVE

A child who lives with criticism is a good example of this.

He learns what to do.

If a parent is hostile to a child,

He learns fight.

It is a shameful thing for a child to live with ridicule.

He is shy.

If a child has tolerance,

He learns patience.

Encouragement can make a child's life easier.

He is able to have confidence.

If a child lives in praise,

He is now able to appreciate.

A child that lives with fairness can be successful

He learns the importance of justice.

It is possible for a child to live with security.

He learns to have faith.

Approval is the best thing for a child.

He discovers to like himself.

A child will live with acceptance, friendship, and joy.

Learns to find true love in the universe.

Today's lesson is to review our earliest memories and to take lessons from both the good and the bad.

We cannot change the past by going back in time.

We can always look back, and remember that most things that happened to us as children were not our fault.

As children, the effects and consequences that others' actions had on us were not ours.

Important now is to learn from the mistakes and not let them go.

If our children had to experience difficult times or difficult situations as children, it is vital that as parents or future fathers, we protect our children.

As adults and responsible citizens of our communities, we have a responsibility to take care of and nurture our children.

We often wonder what our children will do as we age.

It is their right, and our responsibility, to provide all they require for healthy growth and development.

Insuring that this happens will in some way end violence and poverty, which can lead to people feeling like they don't belong in society or are better off dead.

This day teaches us all to remember and love our childhoods and to care about all the children in the universe who are in desperate situations, such as war and poverty.

Today reminds me that we all are part of a bigger community and can all do our bit to help ease suffering and pain around this world.

Let us all contribute to a better tomorrow for our children as well as for all children around the world.

How do people around you see you?

Gather your circle of friends.

Grupp yourself into two's. If the number is odd, you can have three members.

Ask each other for their thoughts and puzzles.

Then, they will share what they need to know about each others to be able to understand eachother.

Ask the following questions.

* How do other people see me?

* What is it about me that you should know in order to understand?

* What is your initial impression of me?

* What was the first impression I had of you?

* What puzzles and questions me about you?

* Is your partner right about what you say?

* How do YOU feel about how he or she views you?

* What lessons did you take away from this exercise

Today's activity will help you reflect on what you think others see of you.

You may also be looking to build self-confidence in your relationships with others.

The goal of the exercise was to help you understand your need for belonging, and your various behaviours and attitudes as you relate to your circles and others outside them.

How we see ourselves may not align with what others think of us, and vice-versa.

Our perceptions also change from one moment to the next.

Today teaches us how our current reality changes according our actions.

The ripple effect of our actions has ripple effects in every aspect of our lives.

As the lesson was in cleaning our homes and repairing our family relationships, we need to fix the broken ties that you have with your friends, your coworkers and anyone else in your lives.

It's a whole different ballgame!

It is not easy to be successful these days.

Of course, the ratrace and the climb to its top are all part of human nature.

However, today's demands and rules are quite different to those of the past generations.

It is important to keep up with constantly changing technology. Cell phones, iPods (laptops, tablets), computers, and all other gadgets are upgraded every few weeks.

We live in a technologically driven world that is constantly changing.

To be successful today, we must come to terms with the reality that we require a different mindset.

It used to be that we were guaranteed a secure and prosperous future if our school performance was high.

Today academic success does not guarantee success.

Education remains a vital part of the legacy parents can leave their children.

We are aware of so many people who dropped out school to go on to create and lead their Fortune 500 companies.

You don't necessarily have to be the best student in the class to be successful these days.

This is quite good news.

Today, the game rules have changed. It is now a level playing surface for almost all.

To be successful in today's chaotic world, you need to get your head involved, expand your circle and make your mark.

It's time you get going! Make some new deals, hit new milestones, and start your journey to a better way of life.

Chapter 7: Effective Techniques To Bring Success In Your Life

As has been mentioned, any person can achieve success in their life if they put their mind to it and work hard. You can achieve all your dreams and goals. Your life begins when your resolve to change the way you think and act. But what you might not know is that every habit has a direct impact on your entire life. That's why successful entrepreneurs are where you are today. Because they were focused on a single goal with their thoughts, actions and mindsets, regardless of how daunting it might seem, they never lost sight of the possibility that they would reach their goals. You have the power to make your life better. These guidelines can help you do this.

Goal setting

Goal setting refers the act to write down all you want to do in a specified time frame.

You've heard of goal setting before but never really paid attention to it. It is something I would encourage you to do. It is possible to set your goals and make plans for when you want them accomplished. Goal setting is great because it can help you stay on track and motivate you. A goal setting tool is also an excellent way to identify what you want and where you should focus your efforts.

Accepting failure

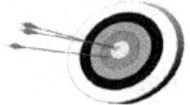

You probably already understand what I mean with accepting failure. It should not mean you are doomed, but instead serve as a learning tool. In reality, failures are designed to make you better and to help you determine the best path for your success in life. Try again next time. If you give up after each failure, you won't accomplish anything and you are unlikely to reach your goals.

Take your chances

The ability to take risks is having the courage to face your fears and being open to the opportunities that life has in store for you. Successful entrepreneurs are those who have the courage and determination to take chances without worrying about the outcome. It is important to take risks when you feel the need. Take the lessons from your failures and learn from them. This will help you find the right way to discover what works. Your success will come when your willingness to try new and unexpected things. You'll also open yourself up to other possibilities.

Working hard

If you want to make a difference in your life, it is important that you work hard. As the law explains, every action has an opposite reaction. It is important to strive for financial independence. You can also live a healthy lifestyle if you want that. Every person reaps the results of what they sow. If your goal is to have a better quality life for yourself and your family, every day should be an opportunity to work hard.

Believing In You

Self belief is key to building confidence in one's ability to achieve anything in life. You will be more likely to fail if your beliefs about yourself are false. Start with self belief if you want to be successful in your life.

These are the most important principles you should be aware of. They will allow you to grow and become more confident. These are the most important things you can do for your life. You'll see many things change.

Chapter 8: The Birth Of The Law Of Attraction

As we know, a law governing nature doesn't have any history. It has been in existence for as long time as the natural environment has existed. Newton was not the first to establish and quantify the law. But it was working in the world even before Newton did.

The history of our knowledge on the law is what we will discuss here. When did people realize they were creating reality through their thoughts?

Buddha was born at 623 BC. He said, "All we are is the result what we have thought." Abraham is an important figure in Christianity and Islam. He is quoted in biblical texts as saying, "All things are brought to you by a powerful universal Law of Attraction, whether they are good or not."

In 1877, the first use of the term law or attraction to describe the idea that "like attracts like" was made. Helena Petrovna Blavatsky spoke and wrote about it while traveling throughout Europe as a philosopher and spiritualist. Prentice Mulford was often credited with being one of the first people to define many of those principles of law of attraction in 1886.

William Walker Atkinson authored "Thought Vessel or the Law of Attraction" in 1906. The term was later used in the writings, in part, of William Quan Judge, an Irish/American spiritualist in 1915, as well as Annie Besant - a British socialist and women's right activist in 1919. The law of attraction gained global recognition as a result of the improvements in communications technology.

The first time the law of attraction really took off was when Jerry and Esther Hicks published nine books collectively entitled "The Teachings of Abraham". They described in detail how this natural Law works and how you can harness its power to manifest what you want.

Rhonda Bryne's 2006 bestseller "The Secret" was published. She talks in her book about positive thinking and the law to attract for your dream life. The book and subsequent film were probably the most influential media pieces to popularize the law.

5 Ways Science supports the Law of Attraction

Because of the internet, conspiracy theories and other information available, anyone can believe almost anything. There are some who are certain Bigfoot or the Loch Ness creature and the Yeti actually exist. They could very well be or they could be a human/animal hybrid. However, their existence has not been confirmed.

This is to illustrate how it can be nice to have scientific and factual evidence supporting your belief. Science has provided many scientific evidences to support the theory of law of attraction. Here are just 5 scientific proofs supporting the LOA.

1 – 1984 Research of Physicist John Wheeler

Dr. Wheeler suggested, for our universes to exist it had to be observed. The observation led eventually to the creation, and even shaped the way it existed. He decided to put his theory to the test on a smaller scale.

His 1984 experiment observing particles in the air suggests that the law os attraction exists.

We will only summarize his research. It changed the particle's state when he and his group consciously observed them. It didn't just change what was going on, it also altered how the particle got to this point.

This is a sign that observation can make a difference in how something behaves and what it looks like right now. It is also a breakthrough evidence that the activity in the past of a particle can be altered by current observations. In other words, it is your observation that led to the particle's first observation.

The law o' attraction states that what you focus your attention to will manifest into reality. You can literally change what happened in the previous so that your present situation is what you want. Your current reality will change, as with Wheeler's particles.

You can become what you believe in.

2 – 2007 Study Reported by the Yonsei Journal

Ji Young Jung is an Korean researcher who collaborated with his colleagues to research the effects of positive thought on a person's personal life. Most people have heard that positive thinking results in positive outcomes. This idea is similar and supports the idea that the law can be used to create a positive situation rather than a negative one.

The researchers discovered positive thinking was linked to greater "life satisfaction". The researchers found that people who felt more positive and optimistic were happier with their lives. These findings are evidence that positive thinking exercises can increase your chances of creating the kind life you want.

Here's the statement that the researchers made about the study.

"These findings provide promise for positive thinking as an approach towards psychological interventions designed to increase life satisfaction."

It is powerful stuff. It shows how conscious thinking can lead to psychological changes that increase happiness. People appreciate the positive aspects in their lives more than they enjoy the negative.

Focusing energy on positive thoughts can lead to a positive reality. Being happy and positive can help improve our moods and allow us to face the challenges of life head-on. Try it!

3 - Mirror Neuron Research

This is another solid piece of scientific research that shows you can design your life.

You have control over your life. Mirror neurons were found in the 1990s.

Italian scientists discovered that a specific group of neurons reacts in a certain way to a macaque monkey grasping an object. This was a minor discovery. Your behavior and actions are influenced by the nervous system. It was however unique that the monkey was able to see other primates grab this object, which led him to discover the same set.

Mirror neurons is the name given to these nerve cell types because they have a mirrorlike quality.

Recent research (the first two decades into the 21st century) has shown mirror neurons to be responsible for certain energies. As in macaque monkey research this same mechanism is used to transmit energy from humans to other people.

An observer who only observes an action is less likely to actually do the action. Monkey sees monkey do.

This supports the law that attracts. Be positive and happy. You'll attract the same actions from others who see you. Positive behavior attracts positive ones. This is evident when people who are fun and happy get invited to more parties or outings. Perhaps you have a larger circle of friends.

But, the law that attracts can either bring you negative or positive results. Your thoughts, energies, efforts, and energy are all negative. You will attract a negative experience. If you are always negative, angry, and mean, you will see this as your reality.

4 - Science shows that visualization can have an impact on reality

To harness the law, of attraction to your advantage, visualization is key. Michael Losier describes visualization as a combination between mental focus, attention, or energy. These are the three components that make up LOA.

Multiple neurological studies have shown visualization triggers activity in some brain areas. Visualizing the desired outcome causes certain brain regions to respond in the same manner as if it were you taking action towards that outcome.

Also, the brain appears to become bored and take little or no action when you communicate what you want. Researchers are still unsure why this occurs. Instead of visualizing and drawing what you desire, your brain responds more strongly to your interest and is more focused.

Amazingly, this causes your brain's memory to store the image you have pictured as something you have done before.

Visualization can have a significant impact on your attention and perception as well memory, planning, motor control, motor control, motivation, and motor coordination. Your brain can be trained to visualize the reality you desire. It is easier to manifest what you want and live the life that you desire if you have mental images of the things you wish to accomplish. We believe visualizations have tangible advantages in realizing your goals.

5 - Five affirmations work to create the desired reality

In law of attraction, affirmations are used. Science is again on the side to show that affirmations are a powerful tool for creating positive outcomes and helping you achieve your goals. Another study from the University of Exeter supports this conclusion.

The Exeter researchers examined the impact of "constructive repetitive mental thought" on future outcomes. They wanted to determine if it was possible program the brain to favor a desired set of circumstances and not just hope that those conditions would occur. The results of the research revealed that people who told themselves repeatedly and consistently they could accomplish anything were more likely to succeed. This could be because the study participants are more driven. However, the evidence supports this.

Therapy clients can use affirmations to overcome depression and trauma.

Chapter 9: Choice

What is a "choice"?

The power to choose among two options or more is called the freedom of choice.

As human beings, there is a choice. We have the ability to choose whether we want to be financially free or in debt. We have the freedom to choose whether we are healthy or unhealthy. We have the freedom to choose to work hard or to not work at any time. We have two choices: to contribute to society or to not. You can choose to either love or hate. We can choose to speak politely and ignorantly. We can choose to either help others or not. You have the option to have kids or not. We can choose to travel the globe or not. You can learn to drive a car, or you can not. We can choose to find a job we love or not. We have the freedom to choose between tea and coffee in the morning. There is so much choice. There are so many options and choices that we can make each day. Only you are able to make that choice.

That choice is made by you. Life is full with many choices. The possibilities are endless and you have the ability to make decisions. You have many options in today's modern age of life. We have the option to choose a husband or a wife, as well as the ability to choose if we want a car, cellular phone, job or lifestyle.

All these choices can be made by you. You have complete control over your life and the outcomes. You are the pilot. It's your choice where you want to go. You are free to choose. Our lives can be shaped by our choices.

We all have the freedom to choose what we want in our lives. It has a profound impact on our lives but we don't seem able to appreciate how libertious our choices are. The fear of making a wrong choice can be a barrier to our freedom. The fear of making a bad decision. It ends in regret about bad decision-making. This is followed by self-blame.

Is it too hard to make decisions?

Many of us would rather not choose and go with the default option if offered. We stop deciding when there are too many options. We do not care what the outcome is, we just want it to be over. Most times, we'll choose the easiest solution. This is because the easiest choice is easy to do. We will choose the safer options.

The greater number of choices available, the greater the chance of regret. We will regret making a wrong choice. We have made this decision from a positive thing to one that is negative. We are afraid of making a high-risk decision. The bigger the risk, so the greater the impact on your life. The greater the impact on lives, we tend to be more out of our comfort zone. This is due to change. Change is uncomfortable. We make choices to keep those around us happy. We don't want our choices to have an impact on the family or its daily routines. We make safe, sound decisions and take no risks. Everything around us remains the same.

It should be a positive choice. We have the freedom and power to control and shape our lives, as well as that of everyone and everything around us.

Choice can have a profound impact on our lives. It determines whether we are successful or not. Why is it that only a small percentage of the world's population lives in a wealthy and healthy lifestyle. And then there are the rest who struggle and suffer. Most are lucky enough to have enough just to survive. Most people live paycheck to paycheck. They can barely survive on a small portion of the pie. The majority of those who survive are only getting a portion of the pie. The good news is that there is enough pie for everyone. It all comes to how you choose.

Choice was different in past times. Imagine a Doctor looking at you years ago. The doctor would have found the best treatment. The doctor would have chosen the most efficient treatment. The doctor would choose the best treatment to make you feel better.

In modern times, the doctor will actually examine you. He/she will find out what is wrong. He/she'll give you a list with possible options. The doctor will inform you about the risks and benefits of each treatment. But the doctor won't make that decision, it is up to you. Even though the doctor has been trained and experienced in this area, they will not give you the final word. This decision will be up to the doctor. The modern world offers many choices. There is little information about it. It controls and shapes our reality as well as our life experiences. It should never be considered negative or gray.

Each decision allows you to create your ideal life. Is this a wakeup? I want my readers to understand the importance choice. Choices can make or break your life. My book focuses on the law o f attraction and how you can create the life of your dreams. However, we must first understand the law of attraction and how to apply it. Understanding the importance to choose is crucial. At the end this chapter, you will have the option to continue reading the book. You can learn the law and attract the life you want.

We are not good at making the right choice.

We make the wrong decisions because of these:

Our fear

Our belief

Our thoughts

Our energy

Our feelings

Our emotions

You're probably thinking right now that these could possibly not affect the final result. A simple example. Would you prefer a cup or two of tea? I would like a cup o' tea.

You were asked whether you prefer tea or coffee. You stopped to think about the question. I would like a hot cup of tea. You must have been in the mood of tea. Perhaps there isn't as much fear because we are so used the question being asked.

Therefore, we need to do all of the above. By doing this, we can make better decisions.

Most of our choices are made by our habits and our normative behaviours. Habits are actions that we repeat over and over. Habits are easier to control and think less about. These habits are automatically formed. They become default settings when you make choices. Everyone has bad and good habits.

We must accept responsibility for the choices we make. Each person is the one who has the power to make their own choices. We don't know how much power our human beings have. We have the power to make our own reality. The only thing holding you back, however, is your lack of wisdom, knowledge, or understanding of the factors that make this possible. Barricades and obstacles will always be present, but you'll overcome them. This book will detail each factor in its own chapter.

I am not going to listen to what you are saying. Think before your speak. You are free to make your own decision. There are no forced choices in life. You have the freedom to choose your path. Now, you have the option to decide what to think and do.

I will help you make the right choices. I will help you overcome your self-limiting beliefs. I will explain how to transform your thoughts and your thought process. The law of attraction will be explained to you. I won't leave anything out. We must, however, be able to recognize the importance of choosing and making decisions.

Individual freedom is our choice. I am sure you wish to know how to make wise choices. To make the right choice, we must change our beliefs.

Our beliefs are shaped by what we experience and what else we see. Let me share this with you.

Answer the question below.

There is more in the universe

A, Dog with a lead

B, Cats following a lead

You'd answer "A dogs on leads". This is because you refer back to your memory. You think back to your past experiences. You recall what you saw. You have probably seen dogs on a leash before. What we did was simply assume that the answer is based on previous experience. We know this because we've seen it.

It can be difficult to change one's belief system. If we don't experience, see or hear something, we don't believe. What if you could believe you will be a millionaire in a year from now? You could probably believe it in your heart, but you won't believe it deep down.

Why would anyone believe it?

Always ask yourself these questions. Always dig deep for answers. You may not believe it because you've never seen it. It is not possible to visualize it happening. You do not have any plans, goals, or actions to make it a millionaire. There is no faith, no knowledge and no belief. You do not have strong confidence feelings, thoughts or motivation.

Why? (Hint) always question yourself

This is because you chose to believe that knowledge is not available. You believe you do not have the motivation. You have made the choice to believe you don't have the goals, plans, and actions. These were the actions you took without thinking about it, before I told you.

You have allowed your beliefs to determine your future. It is not easy to change one's belief system. It won't be easy to change your belief system overnight. Since you were born, the same beliefs have been part of your life. The people and experiences around you can influence your beliefs. If they are allowed to. This is now the default setting. We must override this setting. It is time to build a new belief structure that will help you.

Mariah Carey, for example. What makes her a singer, you ask? Why is it that you cannot become a singing sensation? It could be that she was born with an amazing voice. It could be that she was blessed with a lot of money. Could it be that she could afford singing lessons. No. Mariah Carey is a Long Islander who grew up in one the most poor areas of Long Island. She chose singing to turn her talent into wealth. Celine Dion, the youngest of fourteen children, was also a success story. They come from a modest family. She sang her ways to riches.

Another example is Snoop. He used drugs to get by. He was sent into prison. He transformed his life. Oprah Winfrey grew up in poverty. She turned her life around. Jim Carey graduated high school as a dropout. He didn't listen to teachers, and he let them influence his belief system. Teachers will tell students that education is the only way to succeed. Teachers tell you that education is the key to success because it has been their journey. That is their experience. Jim Carey has proven that you don't necessarily need an education. J.K Rowling spent her first Harry Potter novel on the welfare. James Bond, Daniel Craig slept on park benches.

These are just some examples of people that we know. Just think of all the other people who make a difference every day in your life. Jim Carey, me and you have no differences. All human beings are one. Our choice determines the reality of our lives and how they will unfold. We make the decisions that determine our future and reality based on what we believe.

People who wish to be successful and to apply the law o' attraction want to rush in and expect all of their desires to come true immediately. Learn all the factors that make law of attraction work. This is your first factor. The first factor in our equation is a choice. We need to be able to better understand choice.

Each of us is responsible for our decisions. No one else. It's not up to the panel to decide whether you don't get the interview. It was not your choice to plan it correctly and do your homework. It wasn't the bank manager's fault not to loan you that amount. You should have made a better decision about how to manage your money. It's not your fault. Take a deep breath. You are the one that makes those decisions.

You have two options: read the book or learn from it. You can either follow my advice or be successful in applying the law. You can choose to attract what you want. What you should not do is ignore any factors. It won't be effective. We will now proceed to the next section, which will include belief.

Chapter 10: What are the Vibrations that May be Holding you Back?

"The amount it takes to get you from where are to where want you to be is not the time you spend changing your vibration. You could stop the hesitant manifestation if you changed your vibration immediately. - Abraham Hicks.

The law of attraction clearly states you will attract anything you commit or become attached too. When you think, experience, and interact, you are giving off vibrations that energy. These vibrations can be used by others to pick up your energy.

Positive vibrations correspond to excitement, love. Passion, love, affection, gratitude. Boredom, worry. anxiety, stress, sadness. loneliness, despair, and anger are all negatives and can bring about negative dividends.

Your environment will respond to the vibrations you send by amplifying your energy and reciprocating them. Positive vibrations will produce positive returns, while negative vibrations will cause negative returns.

Sometimes you may not be aware that your vibrations are being sent. For example, how your business is doing, your relationships with your family members, and your health.

It is possible to be conscious or unconscious about how you react to things around. Unconscious responses to triggers can make it difficult for you to get out of your current situation. This is why caution is necessary.

Take the famous anecdote from a teacher who got into a heated argument over his wife.

The teacher was on his way out and the dog, who was innocently resting near the door, was kicked by him. The panicked dog raced towards the dining hall to escape. It accidentally knocked on a table with milk while running. The milk poured onto the floor after the glass cracked and fell.

The teacher then went back to class to complete his teaching duties. He was furious, outraged, and angry. His feelings spilled onto his students. He reacted with anger to any attempt of his students at asking questions or engaging him in a discussion.

Therefore, students began to be afraid of being irritated by the teacher. They decided to stay silent and remain passive. Others chose not to listen to the teacher and reacted with anger. In no time the class was chaotic with a laissez faire mood and pandemonium from all corners.

The story you see above shows how our reactions to events impact our vibrations. The teacher responded with kicking the dog, which ran towards his dining room, to the argument he had heard from his wife. He then brought the same anger to class and caused chaos.

He received negative results due to his vibrations. This shows that the universe responds accordingly to your vibrations. Negative vibrations can be a hindrance for growth.

It is important to identify negative vibrations and how they hold you back.

It is important that you recognize that negative vibrations may be generated by your environment, pessimists, as well as your own drive.

Negative Vibrations Sources

Here are some possible sources of negative energy

Pessimists

Pessimists tend to be extremely clever and influential. They are persuasive. They have a tangible, tangible energy that is measurable. It is well-known that people are susceptible to picking up negative emotions from pessimists. You will only end up spreading the same negative vibrations to others. You can become a prisoner of despair and despair by being unable to control your emotions, such as anger, pessimism, and lack of focus. Negative people should be avoided, as they only bring negative vibrations into your life.

Compromising your Environment

People relate to different environments differently, likely because of their past experiences in those domains. A person might be scared of swimming in the pool after they have been in an accident. People will also be scared of visiting the dentist because they will have to deal with so many needles.

Many people are comfortable seeing their family's home or office. This is because they feel safe. Different environments can trigger different moods. Negative vibrations can be produced by uneasy environments.

How do you find out if you are dealing with negative emotions?

These are symptoms and signs that your negative energy is likely to be holding you back. You should be aware of the following signs if your past experiences with negative people, negative environments, or a negative mental outlook.

You're crucial

The best way to transfer your discomfort is to criticize others without need. Criticizing people will only make you feel worse. It's also embarrassing when you consider it, especially if your criticism is unwarranted.

You don't know everything.

Habitual complaints happen sometimes without your conscious awareness. Most often, it occurs in the head. And eventually, it is spoken out verbally when it is least expected. Chronic complaining can release negative vibrations that can be absorbed by other people. Sometimes these vibrations will bounce right back to your body and negatively affect you.

Your Health Is At Risk

Negative emotions can increase stress levels and adversely affect your health. Stress can lead to a disruption in the body's hormonal equilibrium and negatively affect brain chemicals. Study after study has shown that anger poorly expressed can lead to heart and digestive dysfunction.

You have insomnia

Negative thoughts can keep you awake at night, leading to sleep problems or insomnia.

You feel fidgety and restless

It is due to the buildup inner tensions. It becomes more prominent when you are under significant stress. Fidgeting or restlessness could be a way to release negativity.

How can I change negative thoughts into positive ones?

1. Always Be Appreciative

There are times when it feels like we do not deserve what is available to us. Although our possessions might seem more valuable than our rights, they can be a source of great pride. Sometimes we lose sight of the true value of our possessions. We are entitled. This blinds us from our true potential. It can lead to unjust expectations that others owe your needs, desires, and wants.

Entitlement, the fastest keycard to despair, unhappiness, and negative emotions such as sadness, anger, scornfulness or greed, is called entitlement. Negative vibrations can be eliminated by letting go of entitlement, appreciating all possessions and people around you, and getting rid of entitlement.

Being grateful for all that we have in our lives, no matter how difficult or challenging, will lead to gratitude. This gratitude will be evident to others. People around us will absorb our vibrations, just like we said earlier. You will find people around you who appreciate your appreciation. This is how we can build stronger relationships.

2. Be joyful and remember to have fun

Sometimes your schedule can be too packed with meetings, work commitments, and personal tasks. Sometimes, your schedule can be too full and you may not have enough time for family or yourself. Your busy schedule may overwhelm you. In this case, you may feel more like a machine then a human being. Stress can result from a congested program if it is not managed with caution.

To avoid this, it is not a good idea if you are a very serious workaholic. It causes a buildup negative energy.

Positivity can be defined as looking for the best in life. This includes making friends, laughing, making jokes and engaging with fun activities to break up the monotony.

Some people seem to be reserved towards sarcasm. This might indicate that they are too obsessed with negativity, so their brains are not able to recognize a joke.

A 2016 study revealed that laughter can help reduce stress-making chemicals in the blood. Humor can help reduce the stress response and prevent depression.

Laughing more often and especially at yourself can make you happier. You'll find it easier and more enjoyable to embrace positivity.

3. Show kindness by helping others

Selfishness can be a sign of negative vibrations. Negative people often only think about themselves. They don't have the time or energy to care for other people. Man is not an island. This means no man can achieve success in life on his own. Your path to self-fulfillment won't be possible if you focus on yourself only. A magical and unlikely therapy for losing negative vibrations is to associate with other people and help them.

Positivity can be built by putting others' interests before yours. The person in front you should open the restaurant door. Be kind and open to hearing their stories. You will feel much better if you show kindness and gratitude.

4. Learn to think positively.

The mind, a powerful organ, influences how we think about and act. The thoughts we feed our mind are the output of our mind. Negative thoughts will feed your mind and lead to negative outcomes. Positive reviews will feed your mind and bring you positivity.

Positive thoughts are more important than negative self-talk.

You can use a simple drill to increase positive self-talk. Saying something like "I did poorly in the project presentation" might be replaced with "I didn't present it as I expected but I will do better next year."

It is difficult to be positive. It's a lot like planting a tree you have to care for until it becomes fruitful. It's best to be able to think before talking or acting. This will make it easier to absorb negative energy.

Be Around Optimists

As stated earlier, our energy is absorbed by the people and environment we surround ourselves with. What we take in is how we vibrate. Negative people, who are known for complaining, arguing and using vulgar words, will influence you.

Also, positive vibrations can be emulated by people who surround you. Surprisingly your positive transformation will be mirrored by the reactions of others. Others will love you more and others will turn away. This is a normal response and one you should expect.

Positive people can be helpful in helping you to see your life from a fresh perspective. It's good to have a group with happy people around you.

6. Accountability for your actions

Your thoughts and actions must always be your responsibility.

This is a way to get around reality. It's an enormous burden to carry.

It's best to look at things positively and take responsibility for what you think and how it ends. Acknowledging that you are not perfect is a sign you are ready to make changes.

Accepting responsibility for the outcome in certain situations allows you to be in control. This allows us to influence the direction we want our lives. In addition, it helps to strengthen our emotional well-being.

A strong emotional support system will enable you to look at situations with an open-minded mind and improve your decision making skills. The right decisions can help you avoid frustrations and prevent negative vibrations.

Chapter 11: Attracting and Fulfilling Your True Calling

There are many people in the world. Amazingly, everyone of us have our own purpose in life. It is essential that we find and live this purpose. This is the key ingredient to true happiness. If you truly want happiness, you don't need to be more popular or have more money. Discovering your true calling is essential for happiness. In order to truly enjoy life, it is necessary to invest time and effort in understanding your true calling and then working towards fulfilling this purpose. Finding your purpose will transform your outlook on life.

Honoring your calling is the most valuable gift you can offer or receive. It's what made you born. OprahWinfrey

1) Identify Your True Calling

Have you found your calling? It's the reason why you are alive. Your personal mission. Do you not understand what I am referring to? Take this quick quiz.

What do I really, truly desire in life?

Am I doing exactly the type of work that makes you want to jump

What is the best way to get out of bed in the morning?

What am I doing that I love?

What would it be like to reach all my goals

If you know the answers to all of these queries, congratulations! There is a good possibility that you have achieved "Right Livelihood," as the Buddhists refer. If not, please continue reading. Your true calling is nearing you. Once you do, your life will change.

2) 7 Tips For Finding Your Calling

Most people work just for the paycheck. Most people spend the majority of their income on bills, and very few do things they truly enjoy.

Others are content at work and have plenty of money. The vast majority of people do not have the means to realize their dreams. It is a fact that most people who are successful are the ones who spend the most effort thinking about who they're and where they want to go. After this, they will constantly evaluate and reevaluate their progress in light the truth of who they are.

It is important to recognize that you are truly special and you can be a great success! You were born to do something amazing with your life. There has never existed a human being like you anywhere in the universe. You are extraordinary in your abilities, intelligences, insight and ideas. They make you different and more valuable than any other person who has ever lived. It is your job to discover the wonderful thing you are and then to devote your entire heart to making it happen. Your life might be devoted to a single purpose (like Mother Theresa's in Calcutta), or you could have multiple, distinct purposes. As you learn and grow, each of these will help you become a better person. The path to finding our calling is an ever-changing process.

To truly enjoy life and get the best from it, one must spend the time and effort to understand his or her true calling. A person can deal positively with their feelings and thoughts, and be open to them. To find your true calling, you must take the time for reflection on what drives you and what stimulates you.

(iii) What's my forte?

Things you are so skilled at that you almost forget about them. You might be thinking of...

How to bring groups of people back together

Great at organizing and connecting with others

How to choose the best stocks to invest in

The ability to quote movie dialogue word by word

It's easy to comfort someone.

Everybody is born with inherent talents and gifts. Each one of us is gifted with unique skills that enable us to succeed in different areas. Is there anything you excel at?

Get great marketing proposals

Great at money management

When looking for your true calling, it is important to examine what your skills are. It is essential to discover what you are best at. This will help you focus in the right direction. Be aware of the compliments your friends and family give you. They will let you know what you are good at and help you determine which path to follow.

(iii). Reflection on Past Callings

- What are the key elements to your past success that came from caring about what you did?

Analyzing your previous success can reap great rewards for the future. Because it allows you to learn from both your successes and your mistakes so that you can identify your true career path.

(iii). Remain in The Present

It is vital to stay focused on the present, even when trying to identify your calling. Keep your eyes on today and not the future. Everything we do today can have an effect on our future. Therefore, it is crucial that we remain present and in the now. Because life is lived in one second, there's no need to worry about what the future might look like five years from now.

(iv). Try Different Things

You must step outside your comfort zone, or "safety bubble". Your comfort zone won't allow you to explore new possibilities. This is where the problem lies. You won't discover what your true calling truly is if there is no chance to explore it. Don't be afraid trying new things. You may need to experiment before you find your true calling. Give it a shot and take the plunge into what you think is your true calling. You might succeed and find more satisfaction and purpose in life. Even if it fails, you still have the opportunity to learn more about your self and what avenues you should explore in the future.

(v) Track Challenges

You can track your challenges and find the common threads. When you challenge yourself constantly, you will find that you feel more purposeful about what you do with life. Your lessons are your guides. These are the places where you will need to grow and heal to become the person that you were created to be.

Do you need help finding your self-worth and confidence?

Trust the Universe and trust others

Feeling overwhelmed and hopeless by your life?

These clues can help you figure out what you should be working on

How are you going inspire others

What you have made a decision to study in your life.

(vi) Talk To People Who Listen

It is important to share your dreams, hopes, and desires with people you can trust. They should also listen to what it is that you have. Try to find people who listen and give honest feedback. Even the elderly can provide valuable insight so it is a good idea for you to seek out their guidance on finding your calling in life. They might know of talents that you do not recognize.

(viii). Live Your Own Dream

Learn to live, and you will be able to achieve your goals. Don't envy other people for what you have. You have to discover what your true passions are in life. No one can fulfill your dreams. Everyone has their individual dreams and goals. If you refuse to pursue it, then no one will. This does NOT refer to material possessions. I mean the things you want and the life you want. Do not try and live someone else's dream. Learn your true purpose to find your passion and be able to live your dream.

Here are 7 Tips to Help you Follow Through

Once we have set goals, we know where we want to be in our lives. The actions we take will impact our ability to reach these destinations. You need a plan to guide you. Despite the desire to accomplish their goals, it can be difficult for many to keep their plan alive. Why is this?

Once we have set goals, we know where we want to be in our lives. The actions we take will impact our ability to reach these destinations. You need to create a plan to guide your actions. Despite their best intentions, it can be difficult for some people to follow through with their plan. What are the causes of their inability to keep going?

A common reason why people don't do what they say they will is that they aren't willing to go out of their comfort areas. Humans are creatures that love comfort. Comfort can be defined as safety, security, familiarity and security. It describes the patterned world in which we live, helps us feel calm and secure, and allows us to be emotionally clear, free of worry and anxiety.

We have to be aware of how important it is not to stay in our comfort zone. There are many disadvantages to staying in your comfort area. To grow mentally, spiritually and financially, you have got to get out of your comfort zones. Practice your mind and you will find that it is easier to achieve our goals even when we feel uncomfortable. The following seven tips can help to keep you on track and follow through with your plans.

(iii. Acknowledge what you want and why.

You must know what you want and why. I see many people around who don't want what they want. It's because they don't recognize their desires. These are self-denialists. If you don't understand what you want, you will not get prompted to do so. Clearness is the only way to get to your target. Your goals should be clear. Without goals, there is no focus or direction. Goal setting allows you to be in control of your own life. It also helps you determine whether you are truly succeeding. It's time to set goals and make the effort to reach them.

(iii). Choose What You Love To Do

To reach your goals, you must keep going back to the things that worked. It is very difficult for you to enjoy what you are doing. Your brain will tell itself that it is boring. It is this reason that people quit much faster than they want to. Many people stated that they have no choice. But they are not able to choose what they enjoy. They allow themselves to be bored. It is up you to decide to stop doing the things you feel you must and visit the area that you are most passionate about.

(iii). Take Action

Another problem is that many people don't even bother to start doing things when they want it. Proactivity is key. You have to act now and do something. What makes it all possible is action. Action is the key to happiness, wealth, success, and even starting a new business. A state of action is the key to success. By starting to accomplish your goal, anything is possible. The first step is often the hardest. Once you have taken the first step, all subsequent steps will be much easier.

(iv). Keep Your Momentum

You can only achieve great success if you create momentum. Don't let your momentum die after you have started doing something. You should keep sticking to your plan. Take action and don't let your thoughts wander. Make sure you have specific goals and set milestones. You can reward your efforts. You don't have to beat yourself up for failing. Start small, taking each step at a given time. A vision board or goal vision note can be created to guide you.

While you are creating a visionboard, you might notice yourself taking steps to help open your mind. This will allow you feel more creative and open up the possibility of discovering inner desires. It helps you find clarity. To keep momentum going through the year you must set clear, concise goals. This will allow you to choose pictures and writing to ignite passion and inspire you to make those things happen.

(v). Valorize your Actions and Results

You can review your actions and decide if you should make changes. Keep track of your progress and monitor it regularly. Keep track of the statistics and compare it to the standard. Modify your approach if necessary but don't change your goals.

(vi) Perseverance

You can tell the difference between someone achieving his goals and not. Staying focused and persistant in your pursuit of your goals are key factors. Dale Carnegie Perseverance is key to your success. This trait alone often makes the difference of success and failure. Perseverance is a personal quality that shapes your character and helps you focus on your goal.

Successful people are known for not giving up. You must also possess this quality. No matter what, you must promise yourself that no matter how difficult things may be, you will not quit.

(viii). Visualize Your Success Everyday

Visualization is a powerful way to attract what you desire into your mind. This is according To The Attraction Mantra Strategies. Daily visualization is a powerful tool to attract the right circumstances and attributes for you to achieve your goals. Visualize it as if you're achieving your goals. Take it in and feel it. You might consider adding background audio to your visualizations. It will enhance your attraction.

4) The final step:

Is there a hobby you're passionate about? Do you have a hobby? Did you do it as a child? There's a way to make a decent living out of your hobby, whether it's collecting comic books, building or creating things, or reading and collecting them. You could open a shop selling comics or you could create an online comics site. If you have a passion for something, you are well ahead of others. Now, you need to investigate the potential for making money from this. Brainstorm. Do you have any ideas that don't come to mind immediately? Start by getting out a piece paper and writing down any ideas that come to mind. You can write down whatever comes to your mind. Find inspirations around the house, on your computer and on your bookshelf. Just write them down. There are no bad thoughts at this stage. Note everything and make a list. You can then review them later. Ask around for suggestions and take a look at the possibilities. Ask for advice from other people. Learn from others about their passions. Find inspiration all over the Internet. The more choices you make, the better your chances are of finding your true passion.

Do as much research possible. Research as much as you can about what your passion is. If you've been interested in this for a while, it is possible that you already do this. You should continue to do your research. Do your research on every topic possible. Also, read all the books that are available. Find people nearby or online to discuss what you would like to do for a living. You can also quiz them about their chosen profession. How much did they make? What education and training were they given? What skills were they able to acquire?

are necessary? How did they get their start in life? What are their best recommendations? You will often find that people are more than willing give advice. Never quit trying. Is it difficult to find your passion in the beginning? After a few days you might give up and quit. You will eventually succeed if you persevere, even for months.

You have a passion but you are not making a good living from it. Don't lose heart. You can keep trying and failing until you succeed. Failure is the best way to fail. Success doesn't come easily. Keep trying until you succeed. You want to ensure your health is in good shape. It's always good to lower your stress levels. You feel better about yourself and that will lead you to your true calling. To be stress-free, however, is what's most important. It is important to have a clear and focused mind. Your head does not get cluttered up with the mundane and boring. It's easier to get rid off stress and focus on what you truly want, your calling.

Chapter 12: The Law Of Attraction

Discover Your Creative Personality

Each one of us has an inner source for power. We just need to tap into it. According to The Law of Attraction, like energy attracts the same energy. To manifest power, one must first discover and tap into your creative power.

You have to let go of your old mindset in order to unleash your creative power. It is time to stop sabotaging you. We can be our worst enemies sometimes because we can be hard on ourselves.

To discover your personal power, it's about getting rid of all expectations and limitations.

Concentrate on what you want from the core of your heart and you will be able to create powerful intentions. The key to unlocking your personal power lies in forgetting the past and focusing instead on the present.

You can have it all. Once you have decided who you want be, your life will be filled with passion and purpose. It is about putting yourself first. By putting yourself first, you will see a change in your outlook. Everything you see in your life is there because that's what you wanted. If you want to have a better experience, set better goals and believe they will come through.

Uncovering your power - The process for making changes

You must focus on the area where you want to make changes in your life.

Ask yourself what it means that you can step into your power and realize all that you have is already there.

Believe that change is possible

Now, start forming your intention with your mind.

If you allow the intention to come in, act as if it has already arrived and have just placed an order.

Expect the unexpected. Create a list listing all possible manifestations of your intention.

Don't be too precise. Try to formulate your intention in general terms. You should give the universe a free reign.

Keep an open mind and look for clues. This is the universe's way of telling you that your intention has been listened to!

Keep your eyes on your intention every day!

What kinda of intention did yours create? The more energy you direct towards your intention, the more power it will give you. A vision statement is another way to focus your energies. A vision is a statement that expresses your goals. A vision statement is a description of where you want your life to take you. It also communicates the value and purpose behind your goal. The vision statement will help you answer your future question and inspire you to become the best version you can.

Vision Statement

Provides direction and identifies objectives.

It motivates and inspires you.

Identify your core value.

The creation of a vision statement

Think about where you'd like to be in 5-10 Years.

What do YOU want to become?

How big do you want your impact to be?

Vision statements are written statements that create a path to the future. It provides meaning for your life and inspires commitment. A vision statement can be made for your personal or business goals.

Consider a vision declaration in terms of power or influence. It could be a statement that represents where you envision yourself in the future.

"I am an influential figure in my chosen field."

"I write things and create things that motivate, inspire and excite."

"I will finish my masters in five years. It will give me the opportunity to improve my earning potential."

"I will become an internationally respected leader in my field in 2 years."

"I'm constantly trying to create high quality products that will help people improve and live better lives."

Your intentions are very powerful, and you only have your preconceived notions to limit them. It is crucial to think about who you want and not just what you want. Visualize yourself living your best and most fulfilling life.

How to be Charismatic, Powerful and Influential

People respond more to charisma than to someone who lacks it. People respond to charisma well. You become persuasive, inspirational, and influential. People gravitate to people who are charismatic. They are drawn to you because they trust you, and want to learn more from you. You can be charismatic and communicate clearly in a way that inspires others.

There are many characteristics, traits, and skills that go into charismatic charisma.

Charisma (or charisma) is a skill you could develop. It's about being inwardly focused, being attentive and true to your self. They are skills you can learn easily.

While charismatic individuals are often born naturally, you can train your brain to acquire these qualities. You can be charismatic if you want to.

Optimistic.

Expect to be accepted and treated as an equal.

Maintain a positive outlook on life.

Stand tall and proud

You can practice paying attention to others and looking into their faces.

Take a deep breath and think before talking.

Communicate clearly with passion and purpose.

Develop your own unique style.

Be open to the possibility that you might not be perfect.

Feel at home in any crowd

Practice being present!

The last listed trait, practice being present, is one the most important. Being present means being engaged with others. Giving someone your whole attention is key. Your gestures and attention show that you are paying close attention to your loved ones. You can become a charismatic leader by giving your full attention to someone you speak to.

Real charisma means focusing on the other person rather than your own needs. Being charismatic makes everyone feel special. Also, it's not only about you, it is about everyone else.

A charismatic person is confident. You are more charismatic when you feel confident.

Living Your Dreams

You can live your dreams by living a life aligned with your values, goals, and objectives. The vision statement is your blueprint for success. Once you create your vision statement and live it out in your daily life, you'll naturally begin moving toward your goals.

Get Powerful by Exercise

Do this: Read this script out loud and try the eyes open meditation. This is a great method to increase your power.

Relax and take a deep breath.

I feel peaceful, and allow the sound of my vocal to soothe me into a kind of hypnotic sleep. As I get deeper and deeper into this beautiful state, I speak softly but slowly. As if everything were in slow motion, my body and voice are slowing. I slip deeper into hypnotic trance with each word I speak and each sound I make. My mind is becoming increasingly clearer each day, smoother than the surface of beautiful lakes.

My mind clears. When I feel at peace, it is. I allow my imagination to help me relax deeper. As I speak, the image of me walking along a beautiful sandy beach comes to mind.

As I walk, you can hear the waves and feel the sea breeze on my skin. Deep and cleansing breaths allow me to sink deeper into this amazing relaxation.

I feel the sea breeze gently ruffle my skin, and I can feel the sun warmth my skin. The sun touches me where I have tension or stressed, instantly dissolving any that it finds. This wonderful healing light allows for me to feel a deeper sense of relaxation. As I get deeper and further into relaxation, my stress and tension disappears. I will drift deeper and deeper into a hypnotic trance every time I repeat the words.

I can feel myself getting deeper and deeper down as I start to count backwards from 5 to 1.

Number five ....I feel very calmed.

Number four ....I'm moving down further and deeper.

Threerd ......deeper.

Number two...........I feel myself descending ever deeper now. Then, the next number.. I will sink into a deep state relaxation. And......

Number one ....I feel very relaxed and ready to make great changes in my personal life.

From that moment forward, my mind begins to picture all the possibilities for me and all the ways I could achieve an extraordinary level of success. I am magnetic and charismatic. I align my thoughts to all the forces of the Universe.

I am in the process to discover my own power. This vision becomes clearer with each step. I am crossing the gap between an invisible world of energy, and the world that thoughts become things.

This vision becomes much clearer to me now. I picture all my hopes, dreams and desires melting into one alternate reality. I am now in the future. I am a person of inspiration and determination. I know success comes from the inside, and that I have all of the tools I need. Only I need to add belief and passion to my collection of parts.

I now feel what it is like to live an effortless life. I now take a moment to picture my perfect day. A day in which all my resources are available and where everything is going my own way. I just ask for what the universe gives me and it responds. Everything is easy in this beautiful place. Everything is so easy and unbelievable. I have discovered a new reality. It is one that I am powerfully magnet. I am driven and inspired to create extraordinary things. And I love my family.

After I identify what is most important in my life, I create plans that lead me to the right place. I am open and willing to learn as I look forward every day. I feel content, giving and generous now that this is the life I want.

I am grateful to all the things I have done and have achieved. This has given my life a new meaning. It is wonderful to know that I am always at the perfect place at the correct time, meeting the right people, and having the right opportunities.

My resources are all around me, and my life becomes extraordinary.

I am grateful for all that the universe has to offer and place my trust in it. I have faith that miracles will happen and I am blessed with blessings.

I have created a powerful, prosperous world. I have enjoyed effortless success. I'm incredibly wealthy, and I believe I am being led in ways that will bring me amazing results.

I have realized the power of my inner positive energy and have seen incredible success. I have the confidence to dream big because I know they can and will be realized.

I feel like everything is possible when I tap into that place deep within me. My goals become reality because my energy is focused and directed to my goals.

This feeling was so deep that it began to seep into my soul .... I started to feel this effortless success as a part and parcel of who I am at the deepest level. I discovered that I can, and do, have it all. It all comes down to the power of myself.

Everything is possible in my universe.

I am strong and powerful.

Respect is what I demand.

I have found the unlimited abundance all around and I have been able to tap into it.

I follow the direction of my heart and find my destiny.

I am open for all the possibilities that are available to me.

I embrace opportunities and take action when they present themselves.

Today, I'm expanding my awareness of the possibilities.

I am charismatic and powerful.

I am always honored and respected.

I am today in control of myself.

I am powerfully influent

I tap into my inner power.

I sense something in me is already making an internal shift. I am ready and able to use all of the resources and energy available to me to achieve that goal. I feel as though everything in life has led to me to this extraordinary powerful place. And I am ready for it to be my reality. I am ready for a new, more powerful life.

I now know I am a strong leader and persuasive persuader, and I have stepped into my true power. I have the extraordinary ability to influence others by my words, actions, or influential behaviors. My charismatic nature is apparent in everything that I do. My words, my body language, and my eyes influence people and have placed me in a favorable position.

As I come back to conscious awareness, it is clear that my life truly is amazing.

Chapter 13: What Is a Thought

An electrochemical reaction is what creates a thought. Unfortunately, it is hard to understand these complex reactions due to their sheer complexity. The human brain comprises approximately 100 million nerve cells (neurons), that are connected by billions more connections, the so-called synapses. Each connection transmits around one signal every second. Some compounds are capable of transmitting up to 1,000 signals each second. These signals are then combined to form thought. We don't know how exactly this works.

The signals are transmitted using electric currents. These are composed of atoms such as electrons, protons (electrons), neutrons/quarks, gluons, and neutrons. Quantum physics teaches that atoms behave as particles and/or wave components. This means that, according to quantum physics, an electron cannot be described as either a particle nor a wave. It can only be determined by observing and measuring the electron's characteristics.

Waves have the potential to be all things, because they can become particles through observation. Everything that exists in the universe latently is a wave. Waves emit an electromagnetic field and contain energy. It is no different for our thoughts and emotions. The concept that thoughts are considered to be electric charges while feelings are magnetic charges in quantum field seems very logical. Our thoughts have an electrical signal that influences the environment. However, our feelings can attract other magnetically similar situations. Combining what we feel and think creates an electromagnetic trail that affects every atom in our environment. This brings us to the question of: What do you transfer in your everyday life, consciously or subconsciously?

All experiences exist in the quantum fields as electromagnetic impressions. You can see the pattern of your thoughts in your brain. It is called the "thank you imprint". There are many possibilities for electromagnetic traces of success, freedom, health, genius, and prosperity that exist as patterns of this energy frequency. When you alter your state of being, an electromagnetic field corresponds to this quantum field potential. This pattern may appear because you are attracted, or because you are attracted.

Your thoughts are a form and energy

Music provides an excellent example of how identical or similar frequencies affect each other. If you put two pianos together and play the "C" note in a large room, the other one can also be played and you will see the vibrating string. This is what we call sympathetic or harmonic resonance.

This principle states people will surround themselves with others who are in sync with their thoughts and feelings. You are actually on the same wavelength. Positive people attract optimistic people. Conversely, pessimistic people attract pessimistic individuals.

If your boyfriend or partner is always feeling down, you will soon feel it. You will find yourself "swinging lower" and therefore attract "low swinging" people. Positive feelings and thoughts can also be transmitted to others. Positive thoughts and feelings will increase your chances of attracting happiness and wealth. People who believe in their ability to achieve success will prevail. This can often happen effortlessly, even if the observer is not there. The law of attraction holds that all we think and believe creates our destiny. We feel happier when we have positive thoughts. Positive feelings lead to positive attitudes that will positively affect our lives.

Energy is the opposite of attention

The law of attraction is simply the ability to make things happen by focusing on what we desire. The self-fulfilling prophecy enters play. Our thoughts can manifest over time. They turn into things and become reality. The old saying that you can only believe enough in something is true has full force. If you set goals and keep moving forward with optimism, you will be able to achieve them.

The universe can be incredibly amazing. It is possible to see and achieve everything our minds envision. To get where you want it to be, you have to plan and execute that plan.

How do thoughts become reality?

Our reality

Visualization

Even in an age of instant messaging and e-mails as well blogs, chat room, mobile phones and blogs, communication with your self is still crucial. Your mental, physical and spiritual health are key factors in your success. Understanding the brain's language is vital.

Many scientists know that images are the key to our thinking. The truth is, regardless of whether they contain words or other abstract symbol, these symbols and words can be transformed into images. Most of the words that we use in our internal dialog to express ideas in words or writing are actually symbols that we have in our heads. These symbols are visual, auditory, tactile, palatable, and tactile representations.

It is crucial to remember that our images have a significant role in both helping us reach our goals and conditioning the self-destructive behaviours that cause us to fail. Images that are permanently engraved in the heads of people attract what they are.

Knowing the basics of brain functioning and the forces that influence us can help us hold images in the head that reflect our goals.

The brain is more interested in images than words.

You will never be able to achieve the things you want. You'll only be able to visualize what you want.

It is common for people who achieve their dreams to have a clear picture of what they want. They had a clear picture and a plan of action to achieve their goals.

This ability to visualize is essential for the functioning our minds and the mental constructions of what we wish to bring into the world. I believe trust in our success, our courage and our ability make decisions and recognize opportunity depend heavily on how clear we can see our goals, dreams, etc.

Positive visualization is the ability for us to see what we want as if we have already achieved it. It is an internal process that starts with a dialogue.

If you do not say the word SEGELBOOT out loud, or in thoughts, it is possible for your brain to see other letters than the ones S-E–G-E–L-B–O-O–T. Your brain creates images of a sailing boat. The same occurs when you repeat a phrase that describes an idea or object for which you have already stored a visual analog in your subconscious.

Mental images are also possible in the brain. What image are you able to draw from the words "Yellow elephant and pink wings"?

Although you don't think it took more than a few seconds to make these words clear, you know the picture isn't meaningful or represents anything that doesn't exist. It doesn't really matter how meaningless something is, such as the yellow elephants and their pink wings. The moment the expression reaches your mind it is your responsibility to turn it into a picture. Our brain uses visualization to better understand the world around us. These ideas are literally reproduced. It is crucial that we speak in the brain's language to achieve our goals.

In a visual vocabulary. Let's assume you have always dreamed about owning a breakfast cafe. Instead of focusing only on one business plan or juggling with numbers you should visualize your cafe. Imagine how you will open your cafe in the morning. The first customers are served. You grind coffee. It smells like coffee. It will be tangible.

3. Ask yourself if these statements, which are part your internal dialogue are true or just the expressions that are often used without knowing why or if they are still valid.

Did you ever realize that fourth grade teacher that said you were "the worst creative person in all of the world" was either referring to your lack of creativity at that age or expressing his frustration with you. That was over twenty-years ago. You shouldn't, as an advertising professional, make this statement. Or, in other words, make the statement in your childhood less relevant to your advertising decisions. I guarantee you this exercise will allow you to let go of half the limitations you have set for yourself.

4. The fourth step is crucial. Eliminate these phrases and expressions. How do you do it? It is important to make the decision not again to use these phrases or expressions, be aware of

your communication style, and immediately correct any mistakes.

5. Write down a few phrases or expressions that are true to you and then visualize the images you want. If your negative self-talk is "I am not creative" then you need to stop. I have great ideas. I like to develop new concepts.

When you read your wish statement, keep in mind that it is not enough to simply read them. Faith and conviction are what you need to communicate. An indifferent sentence recited with no emotion will not have an effect on your subconscious. No matter how hard you try, your subconscious can't be tricked. Your subconscious only acts on thoughts that are stimulated and magnetized to positive emotions. Your mind can perceive the true intent behind the words you speak. Recall that perseverance is what the universe rewards.

Perhaps you find it so simple and strange that it seems impossible to work. It will. Do this and you will have confidence in the results. Also, give yourself some time for change. I can assure that you will experience a transformation.

Chapter 14: Harmony. Right Action. and Moving Your Body

The Law of Attraction may be used to attract material goods and wants into your reach, but it can also help with your inner well-being. There are many meanings to harmony. However, all of them blend together in a... well, harmonious way. A few chords are what you might think of when you picture an instrument. They all can be played together at the same time, and it rings together with a kind of effortlessness. Some people find music so important that it can change their lives just by hearing a tune or one note. The band will sound beautiful if they can play many instruments. The chords could bring up different memories, emotions, and strong desires toward someone or something. Harmony can be described as an instrumental definition. What if there are no instruments you play? This idea can also be applied to your inner world as well.

Harmony in your life is possible when you place importance on it. You will get and acknowledge what you really believe to be important and a priority. Do you find that life continues to bring you challenges? Have you ever considered the balance of your life? Are there any cases where a loved one has ended up in a bad place? You have ever interfered with or gossiped about someone else's life. Examine your inner world. How are you doing with meditation? Are you feeling angry or hateful about an event that occurred to you? Harmony can be a combination of our feelings towards others and our relationship with ourselves.

This is a great step towards addressing the problem. I recommend starting your meditation or contemplation practice. You can start by doing a mind and body scan. Recognize the areas in which harmony is lacking and move to fix it. If that means you need to do physical actions, take them.

Harmony is a way to have a happy life. Your relationships, career, financial standing, and personal life are all better because there won't be unbalanced emotions.

Let's discuss some actions you can do to achieve harmony in your life.

Gandhi once said,

"Happiness comes when what you think and say, as well as what you do, are all in harmony.

Your mind is key to creating harmony in your life.

Like I said, hardships have been a part and parcel of human life. All of life has its challenges. Some are less important than others, while others can be overcome. How we perceive these challenges and how they can be overcome is dependent on our perspective. To be human is being born into pain, disappointments, hard lessons. But to dismiss the beauty of life as simply pain is completely ignoring a whole new side to what it means to be alive. However, I can't take full responsibility for what life has given me. I can however say that I'm sorry for what you've been through. I encourage and support you to keep reading, to see the beauty in all of life.

To bring harmony, you must first accept, heal, then believe you can overcome. It is not enough to be strong and overcome. We can also choose to believe in what we have been through, which will help us face the future with greater grace.

If someone can look at their life with even a smile and appreciate it, they have found harmony within themselves.

The perfect life is what we all want. It doesn't matter if you have a car or a partner, or if you have an animal. Harmony isn't just about getting the material things in your life. Harmony can be described as accepting what is available and being content where it is.

Positivity, however, is the key. Although this may sound like a cliché, it's actually a great one. It's easy just to point at the negative, pain, and the thing that didn't work out for you. Instead of dwelling in the negative, think about the positive. See yourself from an outside perspective, look beyond the current situation, and try to see it from a different perspective. You might discover that things aren't quite as bad at the moment as they appear.

Daily meditation is a game-changer. For inner harmony, it is important to take the time to listen, see, and recognize yourself. You can regain control of your emotions and focus on the positive. Meditation will help you take charge of your emotions and give you the ability to be grateful.

What does harmony for you look like? Maybe a visionboard, created once a day, can help you stay focused and remember the meaning of harmony. There are thousands to choose from depending on what you're looking for. A picture taken in the ocean. Are you not a swimming enthusiast? Imagine vast mountains covered in lush green ivy. One way to promote health and mindfulness is to post a photo of a balanced meal. You could put up a family picture to encourage harmony or best friends. It all depends on who you really are. There are no wrong or right ways to envision harmony.

Reduce stressors in the daily life. It takes effort and dedication to be able to focus on harmony. There will be stressors within your life that cause you to do the opposite. Are you a friend that exhibits harmful behaviors? It could be technology. Each day, set aside time for you to disconnect your phone from the world and be present. Family can be stressful. Look into how healthy boundaries you might have in that area.

The Law of Right Action

The Law of Right Action can be compared to the Law of Attraction. The Law of Right Action essentially tells us to be responsible for what we do and say. This law is built on the idea that you should take ownership for who and what are you. Without valuing ourselves, how can we help others? The Law of Right Action calls us to seek out ways that can improve our self value so we can properly see others and accept their worth. The Law of Right Action demands that you take steps to increase your ownership and bring balance to yourself.

You can start by taking the right steps to acknowledge that strength, and empowerment only come from within. Others will need to learn from you how you treat yourself. It all begins with YOU. Being able to use your intuition and act quickly is an important skill when you're trying to live by the Law of Right Action. If others are complaining, misdirecting ownership or causing major harm to their inner wellness, it is best to be patient. Without caring about the emotions and feelings of others, you can easily tell them the truth. However, this would be against right action. To begin with, you must be honest with yourself. Only then can you guide others toward taking responsibility for their own lives.

"No blaming, no excuses!" It's easy enough to say, but not so easy to integrate into your life. What if the car you are driving almost slams into your side? It was their fault. They didn't even know they were there. Or were you distracted by your phone, walking blindly through the streets? Although it is hard to live with no excuses is possible.

Another way to be right is to live in balance. Some people might struggle with self-absorption. Others may only see what is best for them and others will be more focused on the needs of the people around. Both extremes are unhealthy. You can live in harmony by serving yourself well, and also understanding the struggles of others. It will take time to find the balance you desire and be healthy, but the Law of Right Action is a great way to reward yourself for your hardwork.

Did you ever find yourself repeating phrases like "life has its worst", or "there is no point to living"? The Law of Right Action would tell you that you are going to take action. You have the ability to transform your life. You have the ability to quit your hateful job, break up with a partner, or even move across the country. You can change if that's what you want. Ask yourself the hard questions. Do you desire to see positive change in your life? Do you simply enjoy your daily routine, the same friends, and the same neighborhood? It can be difficult because we as humans are often resistant to change. You might not be ready to make the changes you want in your personal life. Meditation can help to release negative emotions and thoughts.

I challenge to you to think for yourself and not repeat that same phrase all the time. Are you finding your life difficult because you constantly compare yourself with others? Are you frustrated that you can't do the job you've worked so hard for? These are the thoughts that will stop you reaching your fullest potential. Remember the earlier discussion about your mind not understanding lack unless you are giving something to it? This is where you can use the Law of Attraction. You can let go of these negative thoughts and emotions to live where you are. Allow yourself to be open-minded and accept others.

Moving Your Body

Both Harmony as well as the Law of Right Action can be described by the act of movement. Harmony involves self-acceptance, and the willingness to give back what you have received. The Law of Right Action refers to putting life into practice. You can move your body in many different ways. It doesn't have to be about running for long periods of time or lifting weights. It could be about moving your body towards your goals, dreams, and desires.

Chapter 15: 'Force' the Universe to Give you What You Want

The items that we find ourselves attracted to reveal a lot of our personality. Note that I'm substituting thoughts here with attraction. We are the residual result of our previous thoughts or attractions. In other words, our here and now thoughts and attraction are what manifest in us. It is amazing to realize that cause and effect, or "what we see in the here-and-now are the manifestation of our preceding thoughts," gives us the ability and power to create the life we desire by drawing in those thoughts in the moment. Attraction Mantra secrets is a stunning phenomenon. Isn't it?

These are the three steps that will 'Force' all things to work for you:

1) Accept responsibility

It is entirely your decision to go through what you are going through. I may be able to discuss your life with and help you understand it. I could go home and start my own lives, leaving you behind. You don't have this luxury. If you want success, you must be 100% responsible for every aspect of your life. This includes your accomplishments, the quality and quantity of your results, as well as your personal life.

relationships, the state of your health and physical fitness, your income, your debts, your feelings--everything! This isn't easy. It's not always easy for us to accept responsibility for our lives and circumstances. It is a mistake to not accept responsibility.

You are handicapped because you have accepted the fact that you will never be able to change the course of events. You are responsible to your actions and decisions, regardless of how you feel about it. You don't have to be saved by anyone. No one is going to give you the best job, nor will they solve your marriage problems. No one can make you feel any worse. If you don't take responsibility for your own problems, they'll never be fixed.

To see results change, you need to make them happen. It is about taking full control of your life and being willing to work hard to get the results that you want. You need to be willing and able to pay more for the results you desire. You must make your life happen, not passively wait for it to happen. You will certainly make mistakes along your journey but you need to not lose heart.

There is a silver lining to this story: While it might seem daunting to assume total responsibility, it is achievable. You may not have had much control of the outcomes of your life up until now, but your determination to build your might allows you to finally live the life you want. Your mortal might is far stronger than any obstacle in the way. While there will be many setbacks along your journey to reach worthwhile goals and you will most likely encounter challenges, it is important that you don't give up on your dreams.

2) Being devoted

Do not believe people who say success is easy. They are likely to tell you about a product or pitch. It's difficult to win at something which you've never done before. But it's all fine. Let's face it, success and failure don't have to be opposites. If you do not succeed, it is a sign you are taking action. If you're able to learn how the right actions are taken, success will be your natural outcome. What is your dream? What are you fantasizing about? What are you longing for? Let yourself dream. You can achieve your greatest dreams, no matter how unattainable or difficult they may seem. It's fine to want the impossible. It's not OK to pretend that your wants don't matter.

Take it one step at the time. If you have failed, be patient. If you want to achieve a goal that truly matters, such as one that nearly brings your to tears, then you need to persevere. You must never give up no matter how difficult the task may seem. Do not push yourself to become a great leader. Simply do what you can. Your best, at first, may not be much better than total half-wit. You'll gain some basic competence sooner or later. Later, you'll be called an authority by people. This is because they have had enough success to call themselves an authority. It's inspiring to see individuals overcome one failure after the other without giving up. Although it might seem impossible, from the outside looking in, they may be able to succeed. But they continue to fight.

Finally they realize what they have to do. They manage to align their hopes and expectations with the reality of their lives, and finally they see the results. It amazes me to see people who are bound for greatness. No one else does. The sign that is most telling is persistence. Do not settle for less than what you desire if you are clear on your goals. You have to accept that success will take time.

Free yourself of the fast and simple, something-for-nothing mentality.

3) Law Of Visualization

Did you know that thoughts are pure energy? If you have ever had a song stuck in your head, and the next thing that you know someone starts singing the tune, you might be able to influence them. Our thoughts are transmission signals. The universe receives what you think about. You will start to manifest things if your focus is on one thing. It's similar to the power of concentration. Spend more time focusing on the thing you want to make it happen. Concentrating on one thing is more likely to make it come true, whether you are conscious of it. Here are some examples that show it in action.

Focusing on poverty is a sure way to attract poverty. If you place your attention on love, love will come to you. At the end you will attract what your attention is on. It is clear that we believe there are positive thoughts and bad thoughts. However, the universe doesn't discriminate whether a thought is positive/negative.

Like a magnet your mind attracts, but it also repels. If you don't believe that you can accomplish anything, you will repel it. Repellent forces are created by thoughts of incompetence. Fear, weakness, fear, and inferiority. It is almost as if your thoughts create a wind, which blocks certain things reaching you.

Everything is just one thought to the universe. Focusing on positive thoughts will result in a lot more positive things coming your way. Focusing on negative thoughts will result in a lot more negative things coming your way. To attract your desired outcome, you must visualise your dream. You can start manifesting your desires by knowing what you want. . The emotion we experience is a major part of any visualization. It is important for us to have positive thoughts and feelings. You can attract more positive feelings and emotions if you feel good. A tool to create reality via daydreaming, mental visualization allows for easy imagination and fantasizing, as well as rehearsals. However, the inability to visualize these images can lead to undesirable experiences. For example, the worst fears of the mind are mentally rehearsed and rehearsed.

(iii) Create A Vision Board

Write down your goals. Find images that will match them. Use magazines to create your vision board. Take out the words, images and phrases that resonate with. Your vision boards are meant to bring the ideas and images on them to life. It is important to create a sacred space in which you can display the things that you are passionate about.

(iii). Feel the emotion

- Thoughts are the expression of your desires. Emotions give them context. The key to creating alignment between your thoughts and emotions is the key. Your vision board will help you to think as if it is already yours.

Speak the words, "This" and you will be able to say that it is yours. Imagine you want one billion dollars. What emotion will that thought bring to your mind? Are you feeling joy or gratitude for that amount of money. Use the present tense to describe your goals as if they have been achieved.

(iii). Repetition

- Refresh your vision board with new images every day. You will be more motivated and inspired to do the things that bring you closer to what your dreams are. Your ability to visualize and to take action will improve if you combine your repetitive vision with your emotions.

Chapter 16: Where Do I Start?

If you're struggling to find the right place to start or if you're unhappy with your results and want to change, these are my tips.

1) Have more positive thinking.

Negative thinking has the potential to make your life miserable.

Change that mindset immediately. If you are waiting for good news, you can affirm that it will all work out in your favor. But if you do it consistently, you will soon notice optimism become your new routine.

2) "FLOW" positive emotions every chance you get!

Emotion is the strongest weapon you have against struggle, lack, and insecurity.

Begin doing energy sessions each day to increase the quality of your signal.

3) Be the attraction you desire.

Another super-powerful technique that can help you make changes quickly is BEING the person you want.

This will help you to see the world as abundant and blessed.

The truth is that the Law of Attraction can be very easy to use.

You will eventually find a point in your life where you pause and take a look back to see how much you have changed.

Chapter 17: Create the Love You Deserve

How can you find your ideal companion, your best friend, and lover in one perfect package of beautiful hair? And eyes so deep! We've all heard it before, but the truth is that the only way to find the love of your dreams is with yourself and what you see in the mirror. It is your responsibility to find the right partner if you wish to attract them. To attract the best companion for you, you need to be desirable. Confidence is essential to know what you are worth. You can't expect to be productive if your day starts with little faith in yourself. I'm not saying you should let your hair down or not be yourself, but first impressions count and you never really know when "the right one" will come into your life.

It is time to acknowledge your power and stop listening or allowing others to dictate what you think. Knowing exactly what you want, who your values are and what you expect from life will make you irresistible to the right person who will help you get there. You will be able to influence the perceptions of everyone around you from the moment your wake up. Take the time to look after yourself every morning. This includes your hair, nails, clothes, and shoes. True, real men use shampoo and hair products. Don't be fooled by the mass.

It is important to make it clear that you are concerned about how your image is perceived by the world. People will find you attractive because they want to see you shining so brightly. It is not easy to love someone you love and hold them up if they feel self-pity. Do you not believe me? Answer this question. You will be more likely to meet someone for breakfast at work if they are the unwashed, unwashed, sleepy, or confident, successful person waiting for their coffee.

This is not intended to make you feel bad about yourself or to let you believe that you can't live up all the expectations you have from the rest. If you want to attract the love of your choice, then you must have positive attitudes towards love. Only then will you receive positive love from the universe. I think you truly do get what it takes to be loved in this world. Never let anyone make you feel inferior. Accept any opportunity to love someone and show patience for them. Do not be satisfied with someone and think they are the best. Don't push away love for fear of being hurt by someone else. We all have done it. We might run from love because our parents didn't work out after twenty happy years, or because all our exes failed us and we never told them. Or maybe because we don't think we deserve the love we receive. Your past or your childhood views of love should not be a factor in the relationships that you have with others. If you allow your history to determine your future, you are missing the real power of the Law of Attraction. It is about making positive life changes now, not waiting for the future. It knows that you can receive the love and support you need whenever you're ready, without judgments or expectations.

They believe that no matter what we do, we will always marry our parents. That's near the most dangerous thing in this world. It is similar to bad boy bands coming in on your way and clowns at a childhood birthday party trying squirt your with water from a squirting plastic flower that has been pinned to a brightly colored suit. What do we think we should believe? To assume that our life experiences up until this point are the final word, that we will accept whatever fate throws our way. Love is the most important aspect our lives. It is something we can still control. The person that we choose to be our love for the rest our lives should be carefully selected. They should also fulfill all the balances in our universe just as we should. Be the one to choose the love that is best for you, the love that has been in your head since childhood. The universe will tell you that you will not accept any kind of love it offers, but you will accept the best. If you're ready to believe in the Law of Attraction you can achieve this.

Conclusion

The Law of Attraction works on the principle of energy. This means that everything is energy. All things have a vibratory. You attract like energies. Your thoughts, feelings, and vibrations create them.

This information will enable you to change your life. To have more money, power, or respect, all that is required is to train your mind so you think like someone who already enjoys power, money and respect.

These techniques can transform the way you think and consequently your life.

In summary, the following are the basic steps of the Law of Attraction.

Identify Your Desire.

Give Your Desire Attention.

Allow and Receive

Remember to keep your commitment when using the Law of Attraction. It is possible to make improvements in your life by committing to this process. These tools will help you to be consistent, repetitive and have a single focus toward your goals.

Similar to how meditation uses the idea a single point or focus to empty the head, you use the idea to direct the mind in the new positive direction.

The Law of Attraction may seem like an amazing thing, but it's easy for people to get overwhelmed. These tools have incredible power and are made even more powerful with dedicated practice.

There are many strategies you can use in order to realize your dreams. This book will provide you with the basic tools to help you achieve all you want in life: money, power and respect.

www.ingramcontent.com/pod-product-compliance
Lightning Source LLC
Chambersburg PA
CBHW050405120526
44590CB00015B/1832